From One Mother to Another

Uplifting Love Letters from Our Hearts to Yours

K. LaFleur-Anders
Kristan LeBaron
Queen Brown
Tracey Cousin
Juanita Coverson
Jenny Dombroski
Jennifer Dungey
Krystal Grimes
Patrice Hernandez
Kimberly Holiday
Eva Johnson
Monique Johnson

Thelma Jones
Dr. Joynetta Bell Kelly
Rebecca Powe
Cat Rainwater
Andrea Sam
Audrey Stevens
Cyrenna Villegas
Tosha Washington
Jenny Watt
Janifer Wheeler
Sabia Williams
Jillian Wilson

Copyright © 2022 Chestnut Publishing House, LLC. All rights reserved. No part of this book may be reproduced, or stored in a retrieval system, or transmitted in any form or by any means, electronic, mechanical, photocopying, recording, or otherwise, without express written permission of the publisher.

ISBN-13: 9780578292021

Cover design by: Olinart

A Mom's Message Of Hope Despite Tragedy 1
Blessed Is The One Who Finds Wisdom 6
Breaking Free From Societal Expectations 14
To The Mama Of A Child With Special Needs 19
A Love Note 26
Here Is To Celebrating Yourself, Beautiful Queen! 27
The Fifth Louise 37
The Messy Middle 41
Society's Depiction Of Who You "Should Be" As A Mom 48
A Love Note 51
Dear Sister Who Has Been Betrayed by Her Intimate Partner 52
Lessons I've Learned On Being A Mom 55
A Love Note 58
Tirelessly 59
A Love Letter From Mom 63
My Son Knew: I Did Not Love Him 67
A Love Note 73
Beyond Gratitude: For My Mom, Sumai 74
"10,9,8,7,6,5,4,3,2,1 Breathe, You Got This" 79
There Is Power In Asking For Help 83
Embrace Your Village 89
A Love Note from Mom To J and K 93
Encouraging Letter To An Amazing Mom 95
To The Mom Struggling With Working-Mom Guilt 100

A Mom's Message Of Hope Despite Tragedy

By Andrea Sam

As moms, we want what's best for our kids. We want to make the best decisions for them and give them all the tools they need to be the best they can be when they grow up and become adults. Unfortunately, no manual comes with being a mom. We don't always make the right or best decisions. When our kids are born, most of us have a natural instinct that kicks in, and we just know what to do. But some don't have that instinct and don't intuitively know what to do.

I always thought about how I was treated as a kid, whether good or bad. I knew I'd want my kids to have that same good feeling that some of those adults gave me, and I also remembered the ones who weren't very nice to me, and I knew I would never treat my kids that way.

After losing my husband on October 5, 2006, I became a widowed mother at the age of 31, with two boys and a girl to raise. They were ages 13, seven, and three. I was terrified, and I wanted my kids to have their father. As young black boys, they needed their daddy. He was a big disciplinarian, and I knew he would make sure they stayed out of trouble and would help them become awesome young men. I also knew my baby girl needed her daddy to spoil her as he said he would.

But God gave me the strength I needed to be mom *and* dad. It was not always easy, but I could hear him saying,

"Don't you let them get away with that." He would often tell me, "Be tough, Mom. You got this. You can be tough and still show them love. Be firm and stand your ground. Make them respect you." That stuck with me through the years. It was tough, but they respected me and still do today.

My kids loved playing sports, and they knew if they didn't have the grades, they would not play. We missed a lot of family functions due to their sports. Many family and friends would comment about us always missing family time because of their sports, but I knew this was something they loved. I loved watching them, and I knew if they did what they loved, I could keep them out of trouble.

At one point, I had all three of them playing at one time. My oldest son was playing football, basketball, and baseball in high school. My middle son was playing football, basketball, and running track in middle school. And my daughter was in elementary school playing basketball and softball. I was a busy mom, but I never complained. Sometimes I didn't know how I would make all three events in a week or even sometimes in a day, but I did it.

Financially I didn't know how I would pay bills. I had extensions every month for a long time — late fees nearly every month and even a few disconnections. I would consider a second job, then realized that I would have to miss a game or two, so that idea would quickly go out the door. My kids looked for me at every game. Mom had to be there.

My oldest played college football and got married in 2013. I was such a proud mom. Then, on August 12, 2016, another tragedy for our family. This one was devastating — even more hurtful than our 2006 loss of my husband. My oldest son, at only 23 years old, died. It was my middle son's first day of his senior year and my daughter's first day of middle school. She was at a new school, the same middle school my oldest son attended.

Their big brother and best friend was gone. My first love and the one who made me a mom was gone. How could we go on?

How could my babies process this? There are still so many unanswered questions that we will never ever know. He was married with two beautiful babies. He just had a daughter who was 20 months old and a son who was six months old at the time of his death. They would never know their daddy and how much he loved them. Every time I look at them, I see him. They sometimes even act like he did as a kid.

It was definitely not easy to move on from that, but we pushed and prayed and prayed and pushed daily. My middle son attended the same college as his big brother. He also played football and wore the same number that his brother did. My daughter went on to high school — the same high school her big brother attended — and played basketball and wore her brother's high school number there. What an honor for them both. Their brother will never be forgotten. We have so many good memories that we keep alive and share with one another.

Fast forward to 2021, my daughter graduated from high school in May. She graduated *summa cum laude* and is now in college playing basketball. My middle son graduated from college in December — my first college graduate. He is still eligible to play football, so he is now attending another college on the east coast for two more years.

I am so proud of them both, and their accomplishments thus far in life. I am proud of how far they have come after the unexpected death of their father and brother. They don't even know that their strength gives *me* strength. They are now 23 and 19 years old. My grandchildren are now seven and six years old. What a blessing!

I gave you a brief background of my life as a mom and what I've been through as a single mom and a mom who had to bury a child. I could have given up, and so many times I wanted to. But I didn't. Is it easy? No, it is not. It's a daily struggle. My children and grandchildren have kept me sane all these years. Every time I've wanted to give up, I look at them, and I know I cannot and will not.

My grandchildren remind me so much of their dad and to know that a part of him is in them makes my heart smile every time I think of him. I still have a part of him here with me.

My middle son looks like him, and sometimes I can't tell the difference when I look at their college pictures because they wore the same number. For his birthday or even his date of death, I will sometimes make a social media post and ask everyone to give me a good or funny memory with him, which makes my day. I look forward to all the stories his cousins and friends share from childhood or school days. I've learned to celebrate his life and not his death on those days. There is a saying that says time heals all wounds. Well, this wound is still so very painful, but God is my stronghold.

    Don't give up, Mom! You got this! You can and will do this. Talk to your children. Be open with them, let them know how you feel, and ask them how they feel. We sometimes want to give orders and never want to hear how they feel. Think about yourself as a kid trying to tell your side of the story or just expressing your feelings about certain situations, and your mom says, "Hush, I don't want to hear it." And you never get the opportunity to say how you truly feel.

    My children and I are very close, and we talk about many things. I am sure there are some things they do not talk to me about or there or some things I may not know about them or what's going on in their lives. We are far from perfect, but I am confident enough to know that they know I am here if they need someone to talk to. They know they are not alone, and Mom will never not hear them out.

    I hope that I have reached at least one mom. I hope that I have given you the will to not give up, to love on your children a little bit more, and to give more hugs and I love you's.

Blessed Is The One Who Finds Wisdom

By Cyrenna Villegas

Embrace these hands and explore the scars, crooked knuckles, crevices, and age spots. These mother tools have seen several years of toil in household chores, widgets, and ways. They've laundered and folded an insurmountable amount of laundry, cooked a plethora of meals, comforted many a friend and foe, and mended many hearts. They've tended gardens both actual and metaphorical and have held both life and death. Occasionally, they've raised the devil one minute and praised the angels the next.

Looking upon them now, I reminisce the chubby fingers as a child and the long slender hands of a young woman that was carefree and not so burdened with tasks and responsibilities, long ago past. Although gone are the days of toy-playing and creative make-up application, these appendages had a new purpose, including cradling faces in their palms and learning to pray more.

Upon my arrival in motherhood, my hands got super busy holding children, grinding through necessary household tasks, and working outside the home. You name it, and my hands were in it, toiling and producing. In the midst of my mothering career, I presumed that my mindless thoughts were the gears and cogs instructing my hands to carry out the deeds resulting in my actions. However, in retrospect and more powerfully, each repetitive task brought a lesson that rooted itself in new knowledge or a fact in my head and wisdom likened to a mindset gained through the understanding of how the world worked around and, most importantly, *through* me.

Little did I know that God was crafting a new being in me and changing my heart as I worked. Slowly, I'd begun to recognize the importance of His presence within my very fabric. Through the labors, He was cultivating a nurturer's heart and, most importantly, curating wisdom. The most poignant I'd like to share.

Change

I've learned that the process of change is required. Change is where growth in character is built. We may consider our lives ordinary but need to live them in extraordinary ways remembering that change – which can be pleasurable, painful, or both, is inherent to growth. I've recently learned that change and growth include the willingness to be forgotten. With the aging of our mothers and sisters, this is inevitable.

Over the course of the last couple of years, my neighbor, whom I've lived next door to for over twenty-five years, began experiencing dementia. Although I was not aware of the degree of her memory loss, it became evident the day I went to deliver a meal.

She opened the door, and we began a seemingly casual and familiar conversation, and afterward, she inquired, "And where exactly do you live again?" Confused by her inquiry and recognizing that I had been forgotten, my growth in grace kicked in. Realizing it would be futile to resurrect her memory of who I was, and concerned that a myopic response would only confuse or frighten her more, I simply motioned towards my home. It was important to be less of me and more of Him in this moment. To show grace and meet her exactly where she was, unfamiliar to me.

Stewardship

We should strive to be the best example to our children and grandchildren by leading in stewardship. The little souls and spirits of today grow into the stewards of tomorrow's generation and so on. While stewardship requires many attributes, it requires selflessness in plentifulness and sharing our wealth.

Some time ago, my oldest daughter and I served at a Christian retreat, and a homeless woman was in attendance. Although I had prior knowledge of the attendee's domestic status, her clothing and the condition of her footwear was evident of her struggles. During one of our chapel visits, my daughter emerged barefooted. As her mother and already cognizant of my daughter's selflessness, I still inquired what had transpired and asked where her shoes were. No explanation was truly required, but her response was telling, "It's OK, mom, I have another pair."

Yes, she had many if not several other pairs, but beyond her physical and material plentifulness, she was selfless. She had shared her spiritual abundance because she was humble and showed love and consideration for another woman with far less. She is an ideal steward.

Commas

Our life experiences are just one big, run-on sentence. That is, until the real period: when we expire. Life is fluid, and things change. No one situation is final. Good things will turn a bit bad every once in a while, and the seemingly rotten will get better. Our journeys are a sequence of events in which we each have our ebbs and flows — none parallel. Sometimes, we are partnered up in the experiences, and other times, we are mere spectators. Until then, it's all just a bunch of commas or markers for change.

Another daughter is facing a life challenge — divorce. She said she never saw her marriage ending, but they've come to the proverbial fork in the road.

Not having experienced a divorce myself, I can see why one would put a period at the end of that chapter — it seems so final. At the end of her stating that they were divorcing, she added a comma. That comma served as her expressed desire for love and consideration for all involved. She requested that her family continue to love her soon-to-be ex-husband and treat him as we have been accustomed to as a son and brother. Her precisely placed comma works better as it gives hopes for the future for them both, regardless of the outcome. Her use of it speaks to the integrity of her character and the condition of her heart.

The Power of the Word

If you hadn't heard, the tongue has no bones, but as the strongest muscle in the body, it can break hearts. Like many, I regret things I have said and have since adapted to chewing my words twice before spitting them out. Now, I would like to be perceived as beautiful if the words I spoke appeared upon my skin. But, words also have the power of life, whether given in encouragement, compliments, or praise. They are perspective-altering and reflective of our intentions and the nature of our hearts. I believe the most powerful words spoken are in intercessory prayer, where you petition God to help others who need it.

Our youngest daughter had returned to her job after maternity leave for her third child. Soon after her return, her employment was terminated with no clear understanding or motive. Obviously, she was startled by this change and nervous about her new employment status. She kicked into survival mode and visited a food bank. She conveyed the following story to me: When she arrived at the food bank, she was met by a man who perceived that she was not okay. He asked her how she was, and she regurgitated the events leading up to why she was there, adding that she was scared. The man reassured her that all would be fine, and then he prayed for her right there. This citizen of heaven stepped up and promptly petitioned God on her behalf. He spoke words of life over here and shored her up.

As her mother, I am beyond grateful to this man, and although I may never cross paths with him, I can only imagine that he, too, is beautiful. Mostly, I am also moved by my daughter's bravery in her honesty.

Ordinary

You may get too busy to get to church, pray, or set aside a holy space for yourself to heal within, but know that God meets women in the ordinary. In many biblical stories, men climb mountains to commune with God, but God meets women at the wells where they draw water for their families, homes, kitchens, and gardens. He will accompany you as you sit beside sickbeds, as you give birth, care for the elderly, and perform necessary mourning and burial rites. He knows right where you are and the very burdens you carry. He witnesses you, and if you open your eyes and your hearts, you will see Him, even in the most ordinary places, in the most ordinary things, and in the most ordinary people. So my story of meeting God has less to do with times of trouble and more of a chance encounter.

My husband and I had traveled to Louisiana with a church group, and upon our arrival, an elderly woman was exiting the hotel, her shoe untied. Fearful she'd trip, I bent down to tie it. Standing up, we locked eyes, and time stood still in an ethereal suspension too perfect for this world, and I knew that I knew that I knew that I saw our Creator in her and she in me. I would describe this experience as incredible, but even that description does not do it justice. He met us there in the ordinary, two strangers standing in a hotel doorway during an unsolicited act of kindness. He is omnipresent.

I am deeply blessed and honored to have shared with you a bit of my spiritual growth that has occurred during my course as a mother. Although time has passed rapidly beyond the teachings, they resonate deeply, and I still reside in the lessons' residue. First, however, there is one final thing I'd like to pass to you:

Scripture

When I feel less-than, I call upon my shield and rampart — Psalm 91. All of it. I find it beautiful, reassuring, and strengthening. God's promises for rescue, safety, honor, deliverance, and joy are in it. The verse I favor most is 14, as it declares God's love and vow of protection. Leaning into it bathes me in heavenly restoration and reminds me to take care of myself.

We are valuable, more precious than rubies, and nothing desired compares to us. Proverbs 3:15.

We often hear that we cannot pour from empty cups, but we must also recognize that we cannot store much in broken vessels either. Therefore, I encourage you to find a biblical life verse, memorize it, quickly call upon it, and use it as a battle cry when you also feel less-than.

Now that all of my children are grown, I find my hands idle, but I can assure you they no longer call up the devil. And when I'm not sure what to do or how God will make a way, I hold onto faith and know that He will. This is His promise to us, and He calls us His Beloved. This is the most beautiful countenance of the wisdom of all.

My gift to you:

Proverbs 3:13-18
Blessed Is the One Who Finds Wisdom
13 Blessed is the one who finds wisdom,
and the one who gets understanding,
14 for the gain from her is better than gain from silver
and her profit better than gold.
15 She is more precious than jewels,
and nothing you desire can compare with her.
16 Long life is in her right hand;
in her left hand are riches and honor.
17 Her ways are ways of pleasantness,

and all her paths are peace.
¹⁸ She is a tree of life to those who lay hold of her;
those who hold her fast are called blessed.

Breaking Free From Societal Expectations

By Janifer Wheeler

Dear Mama,

Before we go too far, let's get the first fact out on the table: No matter how you became the mother of a single child — through choice or lack of one, you are perfect, just the way you are. So is your family.

In fact, it takes a lot of courage to break free from the societal expectations that you must have 2.5 children, or you are not worthy of motherhood.

It also takes a lot of courage to accept that you may not be physically, mentally, or emotionally capable of having additional children. But, guess what? That's ok, too. You are a mom. Nothing changes.

I chose to be the mother of a oneling because of my own experience with miscarriage and a very complicated labor and delivery due to preeclampsia. I lost my first pregnancy 12 weeks in, and was devastated by grief. At the time, there were no guarantees I'd conceive again, so I was thrilled when I found out I was pregnant.

At the time, I didn't know I would choose to be the mom of only one child, but once he arrived, I knew I was in trouble... and in love. It was only a matter of time before my husband and I had a serious conversation about additional children, and both of us agreed that we were on Team Oneling.

Both of us had felt the restrictions that multiple children bring. He had two younger siblings, and I had one. There was never enough time, money, or attention. Neither of us wanted that for our kid or ourselves.

Regardless of nosy-ass public opinion, I believe it was the best decision I may have ever made as a mom. Having a oneling allowed me to do or have the following with less stress:

Stay at home with him for five years.
Get a Masters Degree
Move across the country
Have date nights and weekends away
Get babysitters
Eat in peace
Take naps
Go for walks
Leave him with his grandparents
Take HIM on trips, outings, and adventures
Volunteer through church, Scouts, and school
Send him to fun summer camps & high adventure excursions
Send him on trips to Europe and Africa
Hire tutors
Pay for college with limited loans
Get him a car

This list is not exhaustive of all we were able to accomplish as a family of three, but it is filled with the hopes and dreams of two people who only wanted to love one little boy.

My life as a mom has been easier in many ways because I chose to have one child. It's also had its share of heartaches and heartbreaks. But the constant has been the richness of my relationships with my son and husband. We are a tightly bound trio.

If you are tightly bound and really close, it *can* make it even harder for that inevitable day when your only baby bird is ready (??) to fly out of the nest and embark on their next adventure. We hold them until they can walk. Hold their hands until they can run. Hold them when their hearts are broken, and until they can hold their own. I think it's our instinct to cling tighter when we feel them pull away, but in reality, our lives as moms are just a series of little lettings-go.

I want you to know that letting go can hurt a little. But, it can also hurt a lot. There will be sadness and longing. You might lay on their bed and inhale their smell while you cry so hard you can't breathe.

But you'll stop. Get up. Blow your nose and remember that your child will come back. There's a lot of truth in that old saying, "When you love someone, set them free. If it's meant to be, they'll come back," or something like that. They do come home, and the separation makes the reunion that much sweeter.

I believe that as a mom, the best way to avoid anxiety and worry over becoming an empty nester is to let their wings unfurl all their lives, so the change is not so abrupt or sudden.

I really tried to give my son room to *be*. I tried to acknowledge him as a separate person from me – someone I had the privilege to know and shape, but also as someone who would be leaving one day.

I guess what I'm trying to say is that planning for the empty nest helps. Giving them opportunities to solve problems, meet new people and explore the world around them *without you* helps. They learn to trust themselves - and you - when you let them make mistakes and learn from their failure. Their confidence grows. Knowing your kid can wash their own clothes, change a tire and balance their bank accounts is important. Life skills give you peace of mind!

Helping your kid be independent is also good for you. Not just for self-care but also to rediscover that you are a *person*, not just so-and-so's mom. You had hopes and dreams. Now you can realize them. It's scary and exciting and scary, but exciting!

But, it can be done, and that's what I want you to know. You are more than a mom. The empty nest doesn't mean you failed or that you don't have anything. You do. Yourself. And your kid. Your kid comes back. Your kid always needs money.

If you've gotten disconnected from your younger self, meet that badass for coffee. Remind yourself of what makes you remarkable! Brainstorm a list of new ideas for hobbies, trips, jobs, books to read, etc. It takes time to put yourself on the front burner. START EARLY!

It took me a minute to figure out what I wanted to do with myself after my son left home. But luckily, I knew this day was coming. I wasn't surprised or shocked. I was ready. I had made sure he was independent, and so was I.

I decided to quit public education and start a digital online business academy focusing on #JOYFullProductivity. I now do what I enjoy the most. It leaves more time to chat with my 24-year-old son, who often calls me on his way home from work just to chat, check in, or get advice.

Just because they leave doesn't mean they don't love you. It's ok to let them fly.

To The Mama Of A Child With Special Needs

By Jenny Dombroski

Dear Mama,

Welcome in and thank you for being here. I know your time is limited, there are tasks abounding, and that you've arrived here with just enough to make it. Unwind the muscles around your eyes, release your tongue from the roof of your mouth, take a deep breath in through your nose, hold, count to peace and let those shoulders go with the exhale.

These words are written from years of observation and are meant to defend, encase, and encourage you when stormy waves that come out of nowhere threaten to sweep you under into breathless space. They also are to serve as a reminder of all the beautiful and unique qualities you have.

You're safe, protected, and valued here. The impact of your strength, courage, and love will live on in legacy and lend themselves as examples to teach as you share your lessons along with words of wisdom and solidarity. I am in awe and grateful to have had the impact of your words touch my life. If you can take anything with you throughout your journey, let it be these truths.

You Have Loved At All Times and That is Enough

You heard the term "special needs" in relation to your baby at some point in time and it feels weird and surreal because aren't all children special and don't they all have needs? But it hits you hard and swells large enough to take away your breathing room and you're feeling just a little bit lost. The time has slowed and you look around for recognition of, well, anything but you come up short.

You look back over your shoulder for what you may have missed. Maybe you did miss some of the early things, took a "wait and see" approach, or dismissed comments and the guilt seeps into your pores, clogging and scarring, as it spreads. You feel so overwhelmed.

Let it go, that doesn't serve you here or anymore.

The only perfect person I know is Jesus. Release this perceived notion that you will know what to do at all times without fail. Some things take a bit to figure out and that beauty is only discovered, more defined, and appreciated when you know that it was navigated with unfaltering love.

You Are Worthy, Have Knowledge to Share and Experience

It may seem as if everyone knows what to do except you. Your assigned professionals put you on a road made by them to form predictable curves and stretches. You can go down it and know what to reasonably expect. This can be so comforting and it can feel good to exchange your, "Hi, I'm new here" plan for their plan.

Please give yourself grace and remember that these professionals studied and traveled to arrive at this destination, just the same as you are about to do. Take those same pages that earned a title for them and absorb their value while applying your real-life data. You are living these accounts and studies. Take what you can from them, but don't build on them as if experiences don't differ from one person to the next. The experts don't get to see progress at home, take into account social victories, see old interests fade away, or progress into new special interests and the joy that comes from that.

You have motherly instinct and knowledge and can account for aspects unseen. It is a mighty force and is worthy of contribution. And, with that, you can mold and shape invaluable pieces of your child's treatment plan.

You are an Avid Taker of Roads Less Traveled

We can plan their whole lives out for them if we want to, but to what purpose? I agree, it would be much easier if we could know what was coming around the bend, but life, children, and progress are always ever-evolving and untamable.

But, we plan anyway and sometimes that plan goes completely differently. Maybe a skill, once thought to be easily attained, takes a bit longer to achieve. Is it hard? Yes. Do we lean into it and let it conjure up whole ideas of failure and a tempting focus on forever instead of right now? No, we move forward on things we can still advance on. Because that is who you have been called to be and who I know you are. A challenge comes your way and you, adventurer, are up for it. You are bold and fierce.

You are still welcome to have feelings about it and it does not say anything about who you are as a parent. If no one around you tells you that motherhood is not for the faint of heart, let me be the first to say that I have waved my white flag many times. I mean, I will get up and go on, but I *am* going to cry first. Processing emotions clears the way to progress.

You are The Protector of The Wild Flowers

Finding out that your child with special needs has to fit in the world is like asking a wildflower in the field to stand out against an alluring, if not a bit untouchable, floral arrangement that was carefully put together so each stem shined in its position. It is just as beautiful as the roses with its impactful color and willingness to go along with anything near it, with just a whisper of unadulterated hope. But, finding a place for it can be challenging so you bide your time with loving care. The process of tending your sweet and chaotic wildflower takes patience and growth.

You are frankly exhausted by the growth and wish it would expand someone else's mind for a bit. But, it is yours to have and you go into each new phase loving the off-beaten path a bit more and finding "normal" a better term to describe an expected temperature on a summer day in Texas.

Slowly but very surely, you arrive at the conclusion that your wildflower and roses may not fit in the same places to some. Especially to those who have only tended to carefully curated roses. And, the anger that arises when you try is steadfast and the thousand tiny cuts of their ostracization leads you to want to protect your wildflower even more just to ensure that they do not become like those who brandish hidden and small knives.

You understand that there is room for everyone at the table and that everyone has a skill set to be admired, showcased, and protected. Isn't it amazing that you can give the compassion missing from so many of your experiences and pour it into someone else's? Where do you even draw it from? God works in mysterious ways and the Jesus I know loves those who need a bit more compassion - and who better to give it than you?

Your Advocate's Voice for Education Paves the Way with Illuminated Steps

It is so easy to go on about your life being laser-focused on getting your child where they need to be physically, emotionally, behaviorally, and perhaps medically. And, there will be all available roads for you to travel down with it. The path is your own. But, it is easy to get stuck on a one-way road sometimes, isn't it? You just go about your business with such fervor that you don't notice the ways of others as you go on.

We forget that as we are learning and building, others are not aware of anything different because their worlds haven't seen the shift. We are tempted to walk on, toss their words aside, and watch letters scatter at our feet. But, how will that help future you and families like yours? You, my dear, have been handed the delicate but important role of advocacy without judgment. I know, it is a hard and bitter-tasting pill to swallow sometimes. People can be so cruel in their assumptions and flippant attitudes.

It is tempting to let people sit in their ways as you go about yours. Know that your heart has its mission and is so much bigger than the personal judgment, heavy stares, or weighted comments. You are your child's voice for the right to exist and thrive in this world. Education starts with you. When someone says that your child shouldn't be allowed, excludes them from having a say, or takes on society's view of who your child is allowed to become, that thought stops with you when your voice takes flight.

Of all the things you say and listen to, of all that hurts you, let your words be those of loving assertion. Only you and I can undo years and years of subliminal and societal training that empowers underestimation. Your impeccable locution will reverberate through families and then through their families with the first bold word. And, even if someone is not open to listening to what you have to say and are hearing the words while discarding them at the same time, you can rest easy that you stood up where most sit down. You were an advocate for change.

God's Got You to Get This

Remember, God's got every path, person, and life in His capable hands and He has His loving hand on your back guiding you every step of the way. Reminding you, with His presence and spontaneous thoughts straight to your heart, that you have people you need to meet and give word to, even if they don't stay past introduction. There are people out there that God has whispered to about you, too. They are coming and even if you feel as if they have forgotten how to find you, "Joy comes in the Morning" (Psalms 30:5).

Your belief and faith, even if it is the size of a mustard seed, can move the largest mountain from view. You are deserving. You and your child are made in the image of God and if He wanted us all to be the same, then mama, He would've taken the time and made us that way. We would have been free to go about our businesses all looking the same, contributing the same, with the same job and the same viewpoints.

But, that is not what He did. He thought one of everybody would do the world nicely. He sent us comfort and confidence to be ourselves just by the knowledge that there is not anyone else that we should be. He put us here to complete our tasks and only we can do that. God's love for you and your family is infinite and unshakeable. Stand on that rock foundation even when you don't know what comes next. The view is better from there anyway.

Take good care of you and I will see you as time unwinds.

Ever in your cheering section,
Jen

A Love Note

By Eva Johnson

Victorious Victoria,

A natural-born leader, yes, you are! Born to shine like the brightest star! No matter where you go in life, nobody can take that from you. And believe me, they will try. But I want you to keep your head held high. Your crown may slip, but that's okay. As long as God gives you breath, adjust it and carry on with your day. I know life may get hard, and you feel like giving up, but don't you do it. You got this!

You can do it. Call out to God, and He will see you through it. Then take it as a lesson and a blessing because you made it through the storm. You may be bruised, but again that's okay. You're here now to get through another day! So, I'm really trying to say that no matter what life brings to you, stay positive, stay dedicated, and keep your faith. These are the keys that will help you to fight another day.

Here Is To Celebrating Yourself, Beautiful Queen!

By Rebecca Powe

Dear Beauty,

Yes, you. I know you are your toughest critic and have a difficult time accepting compliments. I have a lot to say, so buckle up and brace for impact — one full of love and advice. If no one has told you today, you are doing an amazing job! I see you over there queening as a single mom.

Women become mothers in many different ways. The beauty of motherhood is in the unique and sometimes shared similarities. But regardless, your life will never be the same. I know my life has been a burst of glitter mixed with irony. Think of it as a seesaw, if you will, or a jar full of multiple colors of sand because it is a beautiful blend of everything you could imagine and more. Stop searching for that perfect balance. That is like going on a journey to find a unicorn.

Let's take a walk down memory lane to when my motherhood journey became all too real, with these words of wisdom I would share with my younger self if I could.

Take time off from work before giving birth if you can. You will let the scary stories other moms have told you creep into your mind, along with the screams of other laboring mothers down the hall convincing you to get a last-minute epidural. Thank goodness for the March

Madness college basketball tournament because it will help you to focus, which is important while in labor. The doctor will later tell you that you were the quietest birth he has ever had. That may have been a foreshadowing moment of your princess being on a sleep schedule within 5 weeks of birth. Now I will warn you, you will end up falling asleep while breastfeeding or patting her back to sleep and you'll wake up seven years later and she will still be climbing into bed with you. "Mommy, just until you finish your phone call…." Haha, I am not judging you. No one said getting a kiddo to sleep in their own bed every night is easy.

Once baby girl is born, you will be in shock for months that God chose you. OMG, YOU GAVE BIRTH TO A WHOLE HUMAN!!! Welcome to the best 'hood: Mommyhood. Your body will never be the same. Pregnancy brain is real. They'll tell you it will go away, but that was not true in my case. I still suffer from pregnancy brain. Now I have to set reminders, make lists, and leave Post-it notes laying everywhere.

Your body will change. Things will shift and you will always feel like you have to use the restroom…wah! You will be exhausted, but the moment you can get a break or have to drop her off with someone else, you will cry and think you are the worst person on earth for leaving your child. Sometimes your child will run after you or stand in the window crying and waving as you drive away.

You will cry, missing your child as soon as you turn to walk away. Then you will cry because you are upset at yourself for becoming such an emotional creature. The excitement of your child's face lighting up as you return is priceless. As she gets older, pickups will turn into her running quickly and giving the best and warmest hugs and kisses possible.

You will produce an abundance of breastmilk but have difficulties due to an old car accident injury so you will get a breastfeeding coach; nothing will help with the excruciating pain; you will stop breastfeeding once baby girl is about 3 months old. Plus your job will not have a mom room to pump. Stop stressing. Baby girl will still be happy, healthy, and extremely smart. This will teach you to be *you* and your daughter's biggest advocate going forward.

You never envisioned yourself as a mother, but here we are making mommy moves. Since the moment you heard the doctor say, "You're fine, you're just pregnant!" you have embraced this journey. Now you are raising a future leader and legend - or at least that is what you tell yourself as she challenges the Jesus in you daily with her witty banter and growing knowledge.

Motherhood is the most challenging, yet rewarding blessing ever. I understand you feel like you let yourself down by having a child out of wedlock. But continue striving to be the best version of yourself that you can be, as you are raising an amazing God-fearing human. Do not worry about the negative words and looks others will throw your way.

Enjoy the miracle that has been bestowed upon you. Stay focused on God. Having a trusted and competent counselor and at least three hours of cardio a week will be a gift. Your post-birth body and soul will be rejoicing. Every morning you wake up and throughout the day, pray and speak words of affirmation to yourself for at least 60 seconds because the mom guilt will be knocking daily.

The negativity will hit from all angles. It will take different forms. It could be you tearing yourself down; a grandparent telling you how *they* parented, then passively saying, "But what do I know? I only raised x amount of children;" another mom thinking you have to implement her advice; or someone who is not yet a parent, telling you what they would do given your situation.

There will be a lot of tears ahead. The girl who once held her emotions in will quickly fade away. You will be annoyed at your sensitivity. Some of the tears will be tears of sadness and anger, but the laughter and happiness will outweigh the bad. Pregnancy is a time when you have to trust in the Lord and lean not on your own understanding because you do not know what lies ahead. Everyone's pregnancy is different. Do not be afraid because God's got you. Keep a strong tribe around you.

No one is ever prepared for parenthood. You will spend years searching for balance, but there is no such thing. Motherhood balance is finding happiness in knowing life is not perfect. It is, when you understand you are not superwoman. There will be tough days. Take some time to reset and give it a try again tomorrow. Loss of identity is real, especially if you have prided yourself as an independent woman. And once your child is of school age, her friends will call you so-and-so's mom.

Be prepared to be sleep-deprived and wish your child would sleep in her own bed. Then years later you will miss those long nights of little feet in your back or face. You will want peace and quiet. I know you are asking, "What is *that?*" Well whatever it is, it will not exist while you raise a child.

Do not rush the walking stage because it will be the end of your alone time. You know those images and videos you see of toddler hands under the door? Well, do not laugh because that will soon be your life. As your toddler gets older, do not forget to lock the bathroom door or you will have a small human standing in the doorway having full conversations with you or sitting on your lap as you sit on the toilet. Your child will play peak-a-boo or pull the shower curtain back to converse making for a very cold shower.

Lock your phone. Better yet, *don't* lock your phone, because you will find the most random photos and videos of your child that will put the biggest smile on your face. When you are having a bad day, look at the videos and photos in your phone. Call to check on your child when they are away.

Leave work early to pick up the love of your life. Get on the floor with your child. Have full conversations with her. Teach her to read and write. Then school will be easier. Let your friends know that if they call and it is automatically rejected, your daughter is probably watching or playing something on your phone. It would be wise to get a Fitbit or Apple watch.

Make sure you are getting self-care. Self-care is not always a trip or a lavish gift. Sometimes it is sitting in your closet with the lights off for 15 minutes. Waking up early and lying in bed. Taking a warm bath or a few extra minutes in the shower. Reading a book. Sitting on the porch. Listening to music. Dancing in the bathroom. Spending time catching up or hanging with your tribe. It is okay to rest so you can reset. Your daughter will think you hung the moon regardless.

If you used to enjoy socializing, that will change, too. You will still want your friends to invite you to events but you will not want to get dressed. You will spend more time trying to come up with an excuse as to why you cannot make it than it would have taken you to get dressed. You do not really want to leave the house, but you still want to be invited to places. You want to feel wanted.

Workout or nightclothes will become your favorite. Prepare yourself to hear your friends say things like, "You just don't care anymore. Are you in a t-shirt and tights again? You look like a grandma. What happened to that fashion-forward and outgoing girl I used to know?"

People will question your parenting and make a lot of blanket statements. "Is your child's father going to be involved? Did you get an epidural or go natural? You are not a real mom if you got an epidural. Did you breastfeed? How long did you breastfeed? Don't breastfeed. Black women don't breastfeed. Do you have a nanny? How can you work and be a mom? Are you really going back to work after 8 weeks of maternity leave? You work too much. You don't spend enough time with your child. You are a helicopter mom. You don't discipline your child enough. Does that child still sleep in the bed with you? Are you dating? When are you going to start dating? Wow, you are very strong to choose to be single and celibate. You are crazy to choose to be single. You are setting a bad example by having a child out of wedlock. Don't celebrate your child: she was born out of wedlock. You are promoting being a single mom." And the list goes on.

Do not listen to the negativity. It will be a tough journey at times. You will be blindsided by the unsolicited comments, being a new mom, mom guilt, and loss of self. If all of that were in a bottle, the label would definitely say, "DO NOT TAKE AT ONCE!"

It is a blessing to push a child out of your body. Many women will never be able to experience the miracle of carrying a child full term and giving birth. Celebrate your wins, big and small. You will never make everyone happy. Focus on your own happiness. People talked about and crucified Jesus, too. Keep moving forward. I am proud of you for learning to hold your head up high as you do your best to navigate this journey of motherhood.

She will not care how much her gifts cost. She will only remember if you were there for her, so do not compare yourself to others. Take time to sit on the floor and play or watch a movie. Travel together. Make new memories.

One of your most honest roasters/truth-tellers will be your child. Be prepared for that same little human that you carried in your tummy for over 10 months, to tell you "Mommy do not wear that dress. People will think there is a baby in your tummy." Once she realizes she has hurt your feelings, she will then tell you how beautiful, skinny, and young you look. Be wary of the compliments, that means they want something. Use their favorite snack to your advantage to barter with them.

Yes, you have to negotiate sometimes. They are humans. They need to learn to make decisions and be a part of discussions such as what to eat for dinner. They have a voice too. This will be helpful in the long run when they need to make an important decision(s).

Please remember that the best unsolicited advice I can give to you and any other expecting mother is to do what is best for you and your child. What is best for one mother may not work for another mother. Let the mom guilt go. I know it is easier said than done but you are doing the best you can with what you know and have. When people offer to help you, take it! Do not be stubborn or scared. Use your time wisely to sleep, eat, or clean when others offer to help you. As my one friend always says, "do not turn down anything except your collar."

Show grace to yourself. The world will have numerous opinions of you. There is no need to add to that negative load. Once you have a good footing on parenting, it is okay to start going for your dreams. You will be surprised how many people will work with you. Bring your child along for the entrepreneur ride. This will be amazing because your daughter will get exposure to an abundance of knowledge at a young age. Take breaks throughout your workday to spend time with your child. Those cuddle and educational sessions with your child will prove valuable.

Continue to visit your therapist and do cardio at least three times weekly. Working out in nature will be therapeutic for you and baby girl. Get a sitter if you can. Use that time to pray, cry, and think. If you are unable to get an hour for a mental health check, wake up 15 minutes before baby girl to pray or put a movie on for her and take 15 minutes to sit in your closet to get a few minutes to yourself. Turn off the electronics. Disconnect so you can reset. Get your small but big wins in when you can.

I know you want to start traveling once a quarter but that will take some time to fit into your schedule. You will be afraid to leave baby girl even once she is past the toddler stage and that is okay. Take your time and soak up every moment that you can with her because time flies.

You will be very lonely as you experience a few of life's obstacles. But know that you are not alone. God will reward you for choosing to focus on Him while making your daughter your number one priority on earth. Life will not be easy and things will not happen the way and as quickly as you like but God will provide. Keep the faith. Pay it forward. When you see a mom in public or are having an everyday conversation with another mom, compliment her. Check on her. Let her know that you see her and she is doing an amazing job. Offer to babysit or have a playdate. You never know what someone else is going through.

Lastly, I love you. I see you. I am amazed by your growth and I am proud of you. You may get knocked down at times, but you continue to get up. Your strength and persistence are inspiring. I cannot wait to see what God has in store for you and baby girl. Here is to celebrating yourself, beautiful queen!

And to mommy's princess:

If I had to go through all the obstacles I have faced in life again, I would do it all 100 million times over if it meant I would have you. I love every ounce of you. Please do not ever be too embarrassed or scared to come to me. I never knew I could love someone so much that I originally feared bringing into this world. I will always be your number one fan and supporter. You have been wonderfully made by God so walk with faith, confidence, and purpose knowing whose you are. I am more than blessed to be your mother aka the vessel God chose to bring you into this world. I love you and can't wait to enjoy this mother-daughter journey with you.

The Fifth Louise

By Jenny Watt

Dear Avalynn Louise,

It is my honor as the matriarch to welcome you to the world as the fifth in the line of strong, independent, creative women in our family who have had the middle name, Louise.

I will never forget the day that you became the fifth Louise. I received a call from your mother's friends entrusting me with the secret that you were a girl. I hoped fervently that you would become the next Louise, but that decision was your mother's to make. When I spoke with her that evening our conversation turned to possible baby names. Your mom shared the names she was considering. I wanted to ask about middle names, but I was afraid I would spill the secret. After a time she said, "Mom? If it's a girl do you mind if I give her the middle name Louise?" I am sure I said yes, but beyond that, I don't remember the words. I was desperately trying to remain calm so as to not spoil the secret. Inside I wanted to laugh and dance and celebrate that the next Louise had been named!

I want you to know more about the Louises that came before us so that you can learn of the power of the name. The first was my grandmother, Jennie Louise. Her younger daughter, my mom, was the second. I, Jenny Louise, am the third, and your mother, Samantha Louise, is the fourth. Each has added her own power to the name. These traits are a part of you by blood, by name, by love.

Your great-great-grandmother, Jennie Louise lost her husband when her younger daughter was two. She went to work, leaving her girls to be raised by their grandmother. She held a highly respected position at an army base in Virginia. She never remarried and in her later years lived alone. She had a very active life. She loved to paint, do needlepoint, and draw. She traveled and had a collection of photographs taken all over the world. From her, I learned strength and independence but at the time, I believed that these were traits that came with age and wisdom.

The second Louise, my mother, was the younger daughter of the first. Because of this, I believe the name is bestowed by design to the woman who would best embody the name and not solely to the firstborn. I like to hope the lineage will continue indefinitely, but I understand a Louise is born, not made, and not all in the biological line will carry the name.

My mother told me a story when I was a young girl about the wool coat she wore. When she was single and working, she had seen the coat in the window of a store she passed on the way to work. She decided she would own that coat and worked to save the money to make what, to her, was an extravagant purchase. Yes, a warm coat is a useful thing to have during winters in Virginia where she lived, but this coat looked and felt like a luxurious fur coat. As a child, l loved stroking the coat and feeling its softness. When I was allowed to wear it when I got older, I felt like a princess in the coat. No expensive real fur coat could match the worth of that coat in my mother's eyes. She was proud of what the coat represented: the freedom and power she possessed to make a life of her choosing.

I was glad my mother had found that power again after her divorce. She returned to work and worked her way up to office manager in the Speech and Communications Department at the University of Georgia. From watching her, I learned the importance of taking back my power after it had been relinquished.

One of the greatest gifts my mother gave me was complete and total acceptance of who I am. It was something that she gave to everyone. My friends found comfort in going to my mom with their problems and life crises. She listened and loved them for who they were at that moment.

While my mother did not always agree with my choices, her love for me was unquestionable. She saw my foibles, my eccentricities, and faults and let me know she saw them. It was not meant to make me change who I was but to let me know that I was seen, understood, and accepted. I have tried to embody this trait in my own life. To that trait, I have added the ability to allow the people in my life the space to become who they are meant to be. It has been challenging to raise the fourth Louise, your mother, in that way instead of forcing on her a version that I thought would be best.

As I struggle to take back my power and independence and to find my true voice, I watch with pride as your mother claims her power, uses her voice and does not allow anyone or anything to prevent her from being who she is meant to be.

While I believe confidence is something you are born with, I also know that it returns with wisdom and experience. I continue to watch your mom embody the energy of Louise in her own way while also displaying the traits that the women who came before her have added to the power of the name. I hope she will find her confidence and claim it.

You are at the beginning of discovering and embodying the power in the name Louise. I already see your strength, determination, and creativity. I hope you will hold onto your confidence and not let anyone cause you to want to limit who you are and what you are capable of. I cannot wait to see how you become your unique version of Louise.

I wish you joy, love, and all that you want from life.

The Messy Middle

By Cat Rainwater

They lied to us. From the sweet and blissfully silent, perfectly pink baby dolls handed to us to care for while we were ourselves just infants to the promise that God would only give us what we could handle. All epic misrepresentations of what was to come for us all in the misadventures of motherhood.

Suppose I go to Heaven, which is highly unlikely as I have a forever list of mom and grandmom things to do. In that case, I want to ask God what He thought when he assigned women the chores and this laundry list: pregnancy hormones, infertility treatments, adoption courts, nursing schedules, soccer practices, middle of the night Lego assaults on our bare feet, and angry teenager's puberty all in one lifetime. I want to see the drawing board on which He determined that women can push an eighth-pound bowling ball out of their bodies, forever not sneeze without a pisshap, survive on stale Gold Fish crackers harvested from toddler car seats and sleep in two-hour intervals for eternity. As my Third Grade Math teacher said to me every single day, "Please show me your work to get to that answer."

Also, can I exchange the creepy pink baby doll for an Erector Set?

From our first year, girls are programmed to feel outward and subjugate our needs for others and do it with a smile sans protest. We carry the glass of water to our fathers mowing the lawns. Our tea parties are canceled in favor of our brother's baseball games. We are taught to silently suffer our friend's sharp and pointy opinions, not to hurt their feelings, and smile at the random strangers encountered in a grocery store, so we don't appear unladylike. Their needs and feelings are to be happily met by us regardless of our mood, wants, or needs. Unfortunately, that's a whole bunch of them and not a sliver of joy left for us to indulge in.

Our toys, games, coloring books, and clothing are all preloaded with feminine fantasy pink frills: play kitchens, baby dolls, and Easy-Bake Ovens. All things to care for, clean, and cater to everyone else but us. Boys enjoy toys that are vibrant colors, flying drones, adventure bikes, and technical car models; cognitively challenging and inward programming to enrich the individual. We are taught to navigate a great disparity of roadmaps to adulthood and not a fair trip at all for every little girl in the history of forever. This lady business game is rigged, and our servant girl dresses are stunting our growth and cutting off the oxygen to our souls.

You arrived at the wet, messy, and muddy intersection of motherhood and chaos because you didn't have a chance to grow into yourself before growing your children. You have been programmed your entire life to un-see yourself but to constantly look for opportunities to lean in and care for others.

Our celebrated pinnacles in life are getting married and having children. All of our curious beginnings and shooting star endings are treated like stale heels of bread, silently holding together the only ingredients of our lives that most people value: our ability to love a spouse and grow humans. All of the other events and milestones that make each of us a unique, vibrant, and intelligent woman never make the scoreboard. If we dare to share them, they will often be met with an irritated sigh and indignant shoulder shrug. It's no wonder we find ourselves crying in the far corner of a closet with the last piece of cold pizza for dinner and four loads of laundry to go before we finally claim a few hours of sleep.

All of us have found ourselves silently struggling in the goo of the messy middle of motherhood, one foot in our family's needs and the other quietly trying to escape to find its way home to what is left of ourselves. I'm happy to share with you that it doesn't have to be this way. You can find your way back to yourself, and here is how you do it.

You, Inc.

The most important relationship you have is with the super fantastic woman you see in the mirror every morning and every time you have to change your shirt. No thanks to the always spitting up baby humans in our care! Your highest commitment must be to preserve your health and emotional well-being. Your children don't need a perfect Mom; they need a healthy and present Mom. So your physical, mental, and emotional health must start your priority list every single day. This means leaning into who you are and growing away from who you don't want to be. So when you tiptoe up to, or pole vault over, the line into crazy town, show yourself a little grace and grab a nice glass of wine to enjoy while you yoga breathe yourself back to your center in the time-out corner.

Championing for yourself by advocating for, and protecting your needs, is not a selfish act, nor is it selfless. Both of those s-words are very unhealthy extremes, damage your spirit and erase your agency. Loving yourself through the messy middle is how you hold enough space for yourself in order to balance all of your needs while equally honoring the importance of each of them.

I said 'through' not 'around.' You grow and gain agency only when you run into the gauntlet of emotions. Hold on tightly but don't let go or look for a shortcut. We have all heard these directions on an airplane, "Should the cabin lose pressure, oxygen masks will drop from the overhead area. Please place the mask over your own mouth and nose before assisting others." Care for and rescue yourself, then you will be capable of doing the same for them. Without you, there is no them. That's heavy to carry, I know.

Cancel Covert Contracts

These are the invisible saboteur wrecking balls of all relationships. A covert contract is when you have an unspoken and unagreed upon expectation of someone in exchange for something you do for them; usually born from fear of rejection, feeling unseen or unfairly burdened. You give up *this* to get *that*: If I don't go to girl's night, maybe we can have a sorely needed family night out. You do X to get Y: If I buy pretty new lingerie, perhaps he will compliment me like he used to. Not a bad negotiation unless the other person or people (your spouse and/or children) are not aware of the agreement and have not had the opportunity to opt in.

Que the emotional circus and release the panicky monkeys. Everyone is going to be mad, hurt, and go to bed without dinner when they unknowingly break your silent covenant and hurt your feelings in the process.

Covert contracts are more than just bad communication; they are traps that relationships will not survive. They cannot survive. When you catch yourself making these super-secret agreements that only you know about, take a breath and ask yourself a couple of questions.

What prompted me to feel that I need to bargain for affection, time, or attention? If I give up something important to me and follow through with my end of this agreement, will I feel ok, or will I shrink even more?

This is the time to dig way down deep into your well of vulnerability and be unabashedly honest with yourself. You are the only person hearing the question and the only heart feeling the answer. I'll go first!

I do this because I have had a lifetime of feeling unloved, not good enough, and underwhelmingly wanted. Roll your eyes if you must; I am also rolling mine. Does that mean that no one loves me? Nope, there are lots of crazy, errrr, wonderful people who love me, see me as amazing, and can't imagine life without me. Ok, it's just my cats that can't imagine life without me! When we make these covert contracts to buy the feeling and safe harbor that we desperately need, everyone goes to bed empty-handed and a little less loved and valued.

Move to the safety of asking for what you need. Instead of doing all of the chores yourself and then being mad that everyone else is enjoying their evening instead of chipping in, say something like, "I am going to wash dishes, and you guys can dry and keep me company in the kitchen. You can tell me about your day, and then we'll have a brownie, how does that sound?". No one is going to say no thanks to that proposal, and everyone will be glad you asked.

Triage

Hallmark does a bang-up job of glorifying motherhood and wrapping it in glittery-pink-lacy cards packed with flowery word salads. I highly doubt whoever cobbles those words of affirmation together is a mother. I have yet to read one that says, "Sorry I wrecked your body on the way out" or "I know you will never sleep an entire night again because you worry about me always."

There are absolutely beautiful, rewarding, and soft places in motherhood. Everyone talks to us about them and celebrates those moments as we should! What about the other edge of motherhood? We are whole mothers because we cuddle the soft curves and struggle with the sharp edges. I want to hold a bit of space for you to acknowledge the sharp, painful, and regrettable parts.

Whether you gave birth, adopted, or stand in the gap as a mother figure, motherhood travels with pain, wounding trauma, and not enough rewarding moments. Not to mention the loss of your personal bubble and freedom to pee without a tiny snack-demanding dictator watching you. Find your respite in the calm moments. They will come, and that is the time you must acknowledge your heart wounds and emotional battle scars. Clean them, bandage them and give them the very same loving kiss that you adorn your children's skinned knees with. Accept that you will make a million mistakes and rejoice in that you will learn from every single one of them.

When your body is crumbling from the pressure of being a partner, career woman, mother, chauffeur...listen to it. Sit still and take a break, or your body will hit the emergency stop button for you. I can personally testify that waiting until your body hits the reset button is not the way you want to triage your motherhood wounds. You will not like that trip, so be careful and intentional with yourself.

Motherhood is a visceral call to protection mixed with pain, a pinch of regret, and shaken with undeniable pure love. There will be days that you will wonder how much better your life might be if you didn't have children and moments that you can't recall having a good day before they arrived in your arms.

When you feel like a rock star mom, a fraud, or treading water in the messy middle, you are normal, and all of those are ok to acknowledge and ok to have.

No matter where you are at the moment, know this: they are watching you for directions. It is just as healthy to show them when you struggle as it is to show them your victories. Your reward for being authentically funny, brilliant, flawed, beautiful you is that they learn how to be a good human and love you for it.

Society's Depiction Of Who You "Should Be" As A Mom

By Jillian Wilson

When I was asked about writing this passage about motherhood, I immediately felt like I wasn't qualified. I didn't feel like I fit the bill of being seen as a good mother. When I really sat with what was coming up for me, I realized that I was looking at the standard of motherhood as society has measured it up to be. When I look at my journey into motherhood, it's very short of society's depiction of who a mother is.

I had my first son at 21 years old, and I was unmarried. I had my second child 18 months later at 22 and a half. While in labor with my first son, I closed real estate deals on speakerphone in the hospital. I was young, but I was passionate and a hustler in this world. I was going to provide for my children by any means necessary. I was a businesswoman who wanted my career and motherhood.

I felt that I could have both of those things simultaneously without giving either of them up, and I still managed to be there for my kids with school, sports activities, and every fun activity that their minds could conceive in our free time. I never felt like I needed to be different while in the mix of things.

But when I got side by side with other married mothers or stay-at-home moms, it always reminded me that I *was* a different type of mother.

While I have accepted who I am as a whole, and my difference in this world and as a mother, I'd like to speak to my younger self and young mothers in this passage to let them know to love themselves and their differences throughout the process of motherhood. Everyone will tell you that a mother is a certain way - that they should dress a certain way, they should give up their careers, hopes, and dreams - but I don't feel as if that is true. We can enjoy all of these things while being mothers. I don't feel like we should have to feel less-than with whichever path of motherhood we pursue.

To mothers who don't meet the status quo of what society has painted a picture of who you "should be," my message is: don't allow this to shame you or take away from your job of being a mother. Being a mother is hard, and it's all about sacrificing and being selfless for another human being to emerge into the best definition of themselves. So often, we haven't emerged into that person ourselves, but we still have to pour into our kids to help them become that person.

I was raised by a strong woman who lacked nurturing skills. It used to make me angry, and our relationship has struggled. But I understand now, and I appreciate and cherish what she has given me. I am a strong parent, but I never forget to nurture my kids as well because I know it's something that *I* always needed and wanted. As I got older, I realized that I also needed to nurture myself, so I started doing just that in my healing work.

I do feel as if a new definition for "mother" is emerging, but there will always be those that shame highly ambitious mothers. However, I'm telling you that you *can* have both and be both. You may have to plan things around your kids' schedules, but it can still get done.

    A mother is so many things, multi-faceted and multi-dimensional, in every way possible. When I think about a mother, the word that comes up for me is *sacrifice*. From the moment that we allow life to form inside of us while going through body changes, health changes, and overall life changes - it all starts the very moment that child is formed inside of our womb.

We make the adjustments that we need to make to ensure that our child has the best care possible. We change our budgets, personal goals, and even our lives to accommodate our children in every way we possibly can. A mother is a true giver of unconditional love to her child. The best part about being a mother is our ability to give to our kids while giving to ourselves and others as well.

A Love Note

By Queen Brown

Dear Mama,

Keep your head up high! God will always lead the way! Always trust in Him, He will never lead you astray.

Love,

Queen Brown

Dear Sister Who Has Been Betrayed by Her Intimate Partner

By Dr. Joynetta Bell Kelly

As I stood outside and felt raindrops gliding down my cheeks, I wasn't sure if I was crying or if precipitation had just gotten the best of me. My new reality had not hit me yet as I watched a U-Haul being packed with all my and my 2-year-old's belongings before heading to a new home.

The familiar kick to my bladder brought me back to the reality that I only had a few hours to settle in our new home before it was time for my oldest daughter to be picked up from daycare. I had to hurry and finish my task through my tears, anger, and disbelief. There I was, alone, betrayed, wet, exhausted, emotionally spent, *but still standing.*

My husband cheated on me, and I refused to stay in our home. Even at seven months pregnant, I wobbled my whale of a stomach around on a cane to support episodes of sciatica attached to my 42-year-old pregnant reality. My husband, my friend, my childhood dream, defiled our marriage and betrayed our friendship. I could no longer trust him. The only thing I could do was leave, despite his insincere apologies and desperation to keep me home with him. After counseling, soul-searching, and observations, I knew that I would forgive him but never forget the betrayal or be able to move past his recklessness and deceit. Days of crying in the car on the way to work, wondering if my unborn child would be depressed due to sensing that her mother was in distress, haunted me every time I looked in the mirror with bloodshot eyes and a face I no longer cared to see.

Blaming myself for trusting, blaming him for cheating, blaming the world for the convenience of it all did not bring peace and further delayed my healing. I learned that instead of looking for answers or finding fault, I had to allow myself to just sit in my grief and give myself time to cry, scream, curse, yell, and question God's will. The guilt, the anger, the fear, the embarrassment all took its toll on me emotionally and cast me into depression.

The day my two-year-old walked over to me and put her arm around me saying "Mommy, it will be alright," is when I decided that I was done grieving, done being depressed, and done being the victim of heartbreak. My daughters had seen, sensed, and heard enough crying and sorrow. I stood up and decided that I was going to be a better example of strength for my girls and for every woman who has been betrayed.

Here I am, two years later, thriving, successful, and although I am still alone, I am not lonely. I have joy within my soul, and it reminds me every day of God's promises. God has blessed me twenty times over from my lowest point with career successes, financial successes, and most of all, the reclamation of purpose, joy, and the stillness of peace.

Love will find me again one day, and when it does, I will not hesitate to let it wash all over me. I will walk into love with my eyes wide open, understanding that it is fleeting for some but enduring for the chosen. In love's wake, I have developed a new sense of responsibility for my daughters and myself.

I will stand firm but allow the chill that a new rain brings to invade my senses and captivate my thoughts, but never lose my calling and purpose. Through it all, I have learned the unconditional love of motherhood and the value of self.

This letter is dedicated to every woman who has endured decisions that were too hard to make. To those women who waiver and wish to cower and fall, I encourage you to stand in the rain, face and finish your task. Stand in the rain and trust your process. Stand in the rain and let it be a reminder that you are covered by God and all His greatness.

Lilies of the field pale in comparison to the light you will bring when your tears are cleared, and your smile expands with every heartbeat of freedom and joy. Live in the light of peace and know that you are loved, protected, and cleansed by the rain that once consumed you. Go in strength, my sisters. Be in peace and recognize your new reality: *life* and the fullness thereof.

With Every Prayer of Strength to you,

Dr. Joynetta Bell Kelly

Lessons I've Learned On Being A Mom

By Juanita A. Coverson

Dear Moms,

Motherhood is one of the most beautiful accomplishments that God provided us with. To have a part of us in our kids is such a gift (and can be a curse too!)

Here are a few things I've learned being a Mom:

Motherhood isn't easy all the time. It just isn't. No matter how many books are out there to talk about how to care for a baby, infant, tween, teen, puberty days, etc., the complete opposite always happens. God gave you the ability to handle the opposite. Never be afraid to trust your gut to do what is best.

Tell them, show them, test them. Showing our children about life through voice, action, and test is just what we have to do! Yes, we were their age at one point, but they go through so much more. Love them through it all, but feel confident in knowing that you're protecting them for life through these stages.

Love. Saying "I love you" and showing "I love you" are two different things. As a kid, I sometimes wondered if my family loved me because I was never told. As I got older, I learned that they all loved me, although they never said it. Let your kids hear it and feel it.

<u>Meditation and Prayer.</u> Meditation and prayer are something new for me and I do both. I read something recently that says, "Prayer is when you're talking to God and meditation is when you're willing to listen to God," and I know that I have to do both. Life deals us a tough hand at times. Outside of being a Mother, we have so much to do in order to provide. Meditation and Prayer are a few of the ways that I find to take care of myself so that I can take care of and love my kids freely and openly, as well as myself.

I have three kids: Myriana (23), Reggie Jr. "RJ" (20), and Jacob (10). Yes, that's just what God had in the plan for me, and at his timing. Does Jacob get away with a bit more than the other two? Yes, he does. And guess what? Does the world get any easier? It really doesn't, so we have to change with the times and our kids just won't understand that all the time. They may not truly understand until they have their own kids, which is when we started understanding our own parents.

I said all of that to say: continue to be a vessel, a model, an aid, a teacher, a therapist, a mediator, and all of those different "jobs" of love for your kids, whether they understand at the time or not.
Motherhood... just the thought of it is who you were destined to be. Scold the child — it's all in love. Teach the child — it's all in love. Nurture the child — it's all in love.

Sometimes we just have to go to the bathroom and cry and scream in that towel because we're frustrated, but that doesn't mean we love our children any less. I went into my closet and ate my slice of strawberry cheesecake because I didn't want to share and what you don't know won't hurt you. Yes, I know I don't know how to dance, but we're going to have fun doing so.

As mothers, we will always be pulled out of our comfort zones, cry, feel proud, and all of the different facets of being a mother. Just know: *you* were chosen for this amazing journey. Congratulations on being a wonderful mother. Celebrate all that you do!

With Motherly Love,

Juanita A. Coverson

A Love Note

By Tracey Cousin

"They" say that being a good mom and wife means to be strong, but gentle; confident, but humble; authoritative, but submissive and supportive; and a strict disciplinarian while being patient and empathetic. Unfortunately, as mothers, we sometimes carry the weight of the social pressures that "they" put on us to be perfect. We second-guess our abilities as caregivers and spouses because of the insecurity we experience when we are trying to do the "right" thing.

I think that being a good mom and wife means caring enough to be willing to try to be better. Just as we develop and evolve throughout our lifetime, motherhood is an evolution that takes trial and error. Sometimes, many errors.

We all face different challenges and opportunities, raise children with unique personalities and temperaments, and have varying roles in our households. There could never be a cookie-cutter "perfect" way to handle a situation or mother our children.

We ladies need to learn how to give ourselves grace and find solace in the fact that we all make mistakes. But if you are doing the best that you can with the resources and knowledge you have, you are doing a good job!

Tirelessly

By Audrey Stevens

Mother of six wonderful children. The oldest is seventeen, and then it goes: fifteen, twelve, nine, five, and four months - and yes, they were all planned. Married for 21 years. I am a stay-at-home mother, entrepreneur, and woman of many hats. Today I share with you a great word that has been dwelling in my heart for a few months: *tirelessly*. "Tireless" is defined as "with great effort and energy."

The back story is that three of our children have special needs. The first child is diagnosed with ADHD; we have one with severe autism, and one that has overcome Apraxia. You can imagine the struggles of balancing therapy, constantly striving for a constructive routine, and maintaining day-to-day education of life skills. Yet, all three of our special needs children have overcome many obstacles.

What is the hidden and unseen factor of endless maintenance in a combined special needs and neurotypical family? Lots of awake hours, forgotten meals, meetings, and long-winded redirection and love. Very different from an all-neurotypical unit. There are struggles within a special needs family that only one who lives it can truly relate. It is a constant war zone. We entered a season when one is just popping out of regression, then faced another jumping into regression. Murphy's Law? I will tell you from my experience.

Picture this: you just gave birth and your baby is now four months old. Out of those four months, two regressions for just one of your children appear out of nowhere. All these years have prepared you for such a time as this, but your heartstrings are hormonal because of sleep deprivation and, well, hormones. You are nursing at midnight and conducting a motivational speech with your oldest at the same time. Those speeches may last one to four hours. This was our experience with our older teenager. No one thing will ever prepare you for when that motivational speech is not taken seriously, and you must watch another day go by, and your wisdom is not being practiced. How do you love tirelessly?

I can tell you. I am rocking the newest baby and persevering what mothers endure. Long nights. Long weeks, long months. The love that is given to the newest baby is the same love that was given to the other children. While one is in his hardest stage of teenage years going into adulthood, a mother's love will make the sacrifice to listen, to feel their suffering and struggles, and attempt to fix all the things. You must enjoy the positives and celebrate them often, too.

In my current motherhood walk, I learned that the same gentle spirit and love my infant seeks and demands is the same love my oldest demands —differently, of course. It may not look like it on the outside, but internally, it is very much the same.

It brings it all home from how our Savior loves us. We are welcomed just the way we are, and there is no safer place for a child to run to but into the arms of their parents, the strong pillars. We may not have all the answers to the struggles of those teenage years or how to overcome the hard morning hours of feeding and caring for a baby simultaneously. But I can say this: you do not have to be perfect. You just have to be a safe place.

How do you navigate that? I will share what will help another mother in her time of enduring with multiple children.

First things first: self-care. Please, mom, whatever you do, grab groceries that include protein, vitamins, and carbs. You can make a good, quick, and easy meal in less than five minutes. Meal preparation is key to winning at eating great in these early infant times. I mostly prepare foods that I know I can enjoy on the go. I know that my cooking can be interrupted if attempted with an infant or not. Please eat a good meal at least three times a day and have snacks on the go. Please do not be too bashful at the options. It's a short time for this menu. I eat tons of tacos.

Second, have a dozen bottles of water stashed somewhere in your room or in the areas of your home you spend most of your time. That way, you are prepared to stay hydrated as needed, no matter how many hours you may be there talking, nursing, sleeping, etc.

Third, give yourself some grace. These are the parenting times that no one talks about. Days can be hard. But you know, days can also be amazing. It is all healthy. It is healthy to not have it all together. It is healthy to reset, reassess, and work on grace again the next day. When you receive that self-care and daily time to yourself to reset, it so much helps you stay energized throughout the days of the unknowns. At the end of the day, you end with a good night's rest, a clear mind, and the energy to be one step ahead.

We can do all the hard work. A well taken care of *you* is a safe place for yourself, your children, and what comes your way. Whether it is strong boundaries, advice, instructions, discipline, or therapy, raising a family is not always sunshine. But you can indeed have sunshine on a gloomy day. Self-care provides you with the energy to bounce from one topic and situation to another. How I have navigated through very difficult circumstances over the decade with special needs children and a large family has all boiled down to this: how I take care of myself helps me take care of others that are dependent on me.

I have seen the deepest hard times of autism. I have experienced PTSD and anxiety. I have overcome many obstacles in my motherhood of seventeen years. It has taken full commitment to not give up. I have lost more battles than battles I have won.

I speak from my heart saying these words, Momma, do not give up. Eat the energy food, take a walk, put on that red lipstick, and take on the day. Keep a structure and balance between you, your relationships, and all children. Yes, it is possible, even if it is shared when preparing a meal or watching a quick video.

You'd be surprised that a moment of care is not always counted by seconds. Just be the space of love. You, Momma, are the environment of love that is tireless. Your love is everlasting and beautiful.

A Love Letter From Mom

By Kimberly Holiday

Dearest Daughters,

I couldn't write this letter to you without considering the type of daughter I have been. I have concluded that motherhood is magical while, at times, a little messy. Everything in between is what makes motherhood the most mystical. Sometimes we feel that there is something to prove, but being a mother is about modeling the potential to live with joy regardless of life circumstances.

Life is a journey, not a destination — just chances we are taking. The truth is all we have now. Each morning when I make a list of all the things that I am grateful for, you are at the top of my list. I pray for you more than I pray for myself. I have the audacity to believe that my prayers of blessings and radical faith will carry you when you have no strength to pray for yourself.

I am usually never at a loss for words, but when searching for an adequate way to express how deep and wide my love is for each of you, I could find no one suitable adjective to match all that my heart feels.

I love you more every day. I am exceptionally proud of the woman that each of you is becoming. Raising three little women to be independent thinkers, dreamers, risk-takers, and realists has been the hardest, yet most rewarding assignment ever given. Even as adults, I will always be your mother. As your Grandma would say, when you age to 99 I will be 199, so always put some respect on motherhood.

If I could, I would still give you the world and do everything I could to protect you from the sadness of your life, giving you all the courage to survive in this world of compromise. There is evil, there is good, there is sorrow, and there is joy. I am obligated to remind you that God tells us we are a part of the world but that we do not conform to the ways of the world. Just be you.

I am proud to be your Mommy, and my greatest wish is that you would be proud of me, too. Oftentimes I get it wrong, blowing my cool, lacking patience by being short-tempered, hurried, and sometimes displaying total dysfunction in my quest to be the model parent.

If anyone should ever write my life story, for whatever reason there might be, you would be there between each line of pain and glory. There is no handbook on parenting, and without the master manual, I will be the first to admit that there have been plenty of times I just flat out got it wrong. Motherhood is messy. I like to call it beautiful chaos. But, there have been moments when I got it right. It was then that I felt so elated with myself that I had to give myself a high five.

There is not any one part of you that you must hide from me, for I will love you always. You are not broken, but whole. You are not the mistakes you have made; you are not the color of your skin on the outside, but your soul is all light. You are divinity defined. You are the God inside, a star, the most important part of all life has to offer.

I have done my best to shield you from the childhood trauma that I experienced, sacrificing in love so that you had the opportunity, safety, and grace to become who you desire to be. The doctors told me that I would never have a child of my own, but God had other plans. Instead, he blessed me with three queens to raise.

Chelsey Marie, you will always be my beautiful surprise, adopted at birth and born into my heart the moment I laid eyes on you. We grew up together. I fought for you. I chose you, and I would do it all over again. When you connect with your birth family, I will be on the sidelines cheering you in love. You are my miracle number one.

Jada Nicole, you are a reminder of the promises God has spoken over my life. He promised me double for my trouble, but He blessed me in overflow when you were born. For the first time in my life, I felt that I had finally gotten something right. Jada, dream big and be willing to labor with perseverance for what your heart longs for. You are my miracle number two.

Andrea Faith, born at one pound many thought you would not live beyond days or months, but I knew what God said about you, *you shall live*. I never gave up hope. You have defied all odds medically, physically, and academically. Even when you don't want it, I will always be your greatest advocate because that's what Mommies do. Being a teenager today is hard, and I know that I don't understand all that you feel, but I will be beside you every step of the way. Follow your soul. You are my miracle number three.

You will always be the greatest part of my life story. I am the best version of me because you love through my good and my bad. If I am a reflection of you and all that you are becoming, then as your mother, I am pretty fly!

Forever is a long time, and that's how long I will love you. We must live our lives as if today was the last day, and for that reason, if these were my last words to you, I just want you to know I gave the best of me. There is no hidden inheritance of wealth, but I leave you the legacy of my love.

You are my everything. You are my reason why. You are my joy. You are my hope, the motivation that acts as a catalyst for pressing forward each day of this trying life. You are the wind beneath my wings.

From my heart to yours,
Love Mommy Kim

My Son Knew: I Did Not Love Him

By Kristan LeBaron

I didn't love my first-born son when they first plopped him onto my bare belly. As all the post-birth activities swirled around us and faded into white noise, it was as if he and I were the only two people in the delivery room. I pressed him to me, my small hand covering the entire width of his tiny back.

I slid him up to cradle him, turning his warm, sticky body to look into his brand-new face for the very first time. My breath caught at the very sight of him. I was in awe. He had a perfectly shaped head and pristine features. And wide, knowing eyes that looked into mine with jarring wisdom.

He knew: I did not love him.

Not that first day, and not even that first week. I've never said this out loud before, and I've certainly never put it in writing.

During those first days and weeks, I felt disconnected from my infant son. After nine months of patiently waiting — pining for this baby — bonding with him as he grew in my belly, the connection and feelings of instant love I expected at his birth just were not there.

I couldn't help myself from thinking about all the stories of women who loved their babies the moment they were born. How they instantly felt the mother-child connection, and immediately felt protective of this precious new person. I felt none of that.

I was out of my league. Unqualified. Incompetent. Unfit.

Something was wrong with me, I knew. All my life, I'd dreamt of being a mom. I had always felt it was one of my life's purposes. And now I was one, and it didn't feel right. I had made a mistake. I wasn't supposed to be a mom, after all.

Weeks later, I would be diagnosed with postpartum depression, but in the days between, I was suspended in a slow-motion free fall. There was no sleeping because I was terrified he would stop breathing. I folded myself into a shell and didn't want any family or friends to visit. I just wanted my little nest of three: my husband, me, and our new baby — which made me feel safe and also even more isolated and alone all at the same time.

My son wasn't nursing well, probably because of my stress, which not only impacted my milk production, but he was also picking up on my stress and becoming stressed himself. I was devastated that Mother Nature hadn't given me the very basics every other mother in the history of human mothering innately held. She'd skipped over me.

My infant son continued to lose weight, which steadily increased my stress, and was more evidence that I was not cut out to be a mom.

Bent into my own mother's lap, I sobbed, "I'll just feel so much better when this phase is over - when he isn't so tiny and vulnerable."

My mom, who, to this very day — even though I've been raising children for 23 years — is still my go-to for wisdom and to ease my mind over anything from "I've started a recipe that calls for buttermilk and I don't have buttermilk," to "my kid has just dropped out of college and thrown his entire life away," patted my back and said, "Honey, I hate to tell you, when this stage is over, there's something new to worry about at the next stage. And then that passes, and there's something else to worry about at the *next* one. I still worry about you and your brother, even now."

As is always true with my mom, she was right.

So - because my motherhood journey has always had an undercurrent of insecurity in my own capabilities as a mom, I'm going to channel my mother's energy and wisdom here to tell you that you are more than capable. You are competent. You are qualified. You are fit.

As a young mom, you'll have moments of wondering things like, *"Do I believe in spanking? Or no?"* and you'll find yourself probably deciding you don't believe in spanking, because it feels like it's more about letting off the steam of your own frustrations than it is about teaching your child right from wrong. And then you'll find yourself spanking your child because you've discovered that's the only way your kid responds and learns. Or you'll spank your kid and then feel even more deeply that you're not a believer in spanking, and you've made a mistake by striking them.

You may decide early on that you don't believe in guns and declare that your son will never own even *toy* guns or make finger guns. Years later, you'll chuckle and remember this bold declaration as you watch your kid shoot targets with a rifle at the deer lease.

Motherhood will reveal to you that you're a hypocrite of ghastly proportion.

You'll wonder at every step of the way whether you're "doing this thing right," and you'll be so relieved to have it all figured out with that first kid, so you don't have to reinvent the wheel the second time around.

Then: surprise! Each kid is different, so you *do* have to reinvent the wheel. Every. single. time.

If your child has anxiety, you'll hear your mom's words coming from your mouth as you tell them, "Yes you *can* do this. No, I don't know if you will succeed or fail. No, I cannot tell you what to do. *You* have to make this decision." And you'll be knotted inside with regret for passing on your poisoned DNA.

You'll make mistakes.

You'll lose your mind and say things you'll regret. You'll hold onto these regrets forevermore, your ugly words seared into your brain. Not being able to take it for one moment longer, when they're old enough to somewhat understand, you'll bring it up to them. You'll want to make it right. Apologize to them.

And they won't even remember what you're talking about. They may even laugh a little when they say, "It's ok, Mom. I'm fine."

And you will know that they are right: they *are* fine. They've made mistakes, too, but - by the grace of God - they're *living their life*. They are resilient. The best thing you can do for them is to love them. That truly is, ultimately, "the job."

Their path may not fit the picture you've envisioned, but it's *their* path. They have to own it. And you have to own it, too. And you'll see it for what it is: beautiful, unique, sometimes messy, and wonderfully *them*.

And - if you're lucky like me, one day, your child will say to you, "I really appreciate you being hard on me about _____. I know I didn't act like it at the time. I hated it. But I appreciate it now."

Keep going, momma. Keep doing the next right thing for your babes, no matter how old they are. You are more than capable. You are exactly who they need you to be.

A love letter to my boys:

Nothing gives me more joy than what I feel from being your mom. I'm so proud of the young men you both are, *as if I had some hand in it*. But the truth is, you are both kind, wise people all on your own. You are both incredible conversationalists, with an uncanny knowledge of current and historical events, and an amazing ability to think of the future in creative and unexpected ways. But your humor and your kindness are where you both shine. I've never met funnier people than either of you.

I'm in awe of how you care for others so deeply, but manage to draw a clear boundary between right and wrong, and that you dare to stand firm in your beliefs, and speak up on behalf of them, even when met with opposition. I hope you never lose this bravery.

May you forever be the very best friends. May you always know you are stronger than anxiety sometimes leads you to believe. And may you always know how very much you are loved.

I love you,
Mom

A Love Note

By Tosha Washington

Let me start off by saying YOU GOT THIS! God hand-picked you to be the steward over His creation. I know things may seem rough at times, but that's okay because you have what it takes to push through. You can get through, no matter what obstacles life may throw at you on this parenting journey. Let your baby know you love them with everything in you, no matter what may happen. These days it is so important to show our children what unconditional love is. Love on them every chance you get.

Sow positive seeds into their lives.

It's okay to read parenting books but go with your gut. You were built with an instinct to know just what to do. And if you feel you didn't get it right, try again. In your baby's eyes, you are the best! And you know what? That is absolutely correct. YOU ARE THE BEST!!

So let go of that spirit of fear, learn your creation, love your creation, and love yourself. If no one else believes in you, I believe in you.

No one is perfect, and don't you ever think that you have to be. I just want you to remember to be the inspiration your baby needs because you are their first role model. So end each night and begin each day with a prayer and watch the magic.

Remember, YOU GOT THIS!
Tosha

Beyond Gratitude: For My Mom, Sumai

By Krystal Grimes

It's a sunny Saturday morning in Queens, N.Y. We're dressed in our coordinating Fila short sets, curls, and baby hair. Ready to see what the day may hold. We head out to Long Island, where the "nice" malls are. We are ready to shop but mostly window shop. We walk hand-in-hand, laugh, and giggle as I look up at you. When we leave, you pull out the disposable camera, and we take pictures in front of the nice cars in the parking lot. I promised to buy us one when I "get big."

My memories of my childhood are filled with "us" moments. Even when others lived with us or when we had a house full of my cousins, you stick out in my mind. Always on the go but never leaving me behind. Even when I was with my dad or staying the night with family, I knew I could call my mother at any point. To your chagrin, I did call…a few times at 2 a.m. for you to come get me because I wanted my mommy or my bed. Sometimes you made me tough it out, but most times, you came. Either way, I knew you were there.

As a pre-teen, I cherished these moments because I got a chance to experience your motherly love. I was also blessed knowing that my mother chose to spend her free time with me. A friendship and bond that I've learned to expect and EVENTUALLY appreciate. These moments have yet to end, even as we've added additional lives to our small circle.

Growing up an only child surrounded by cousins, I always noticed that our time together was rare. We were up late at night watching movies together, doing each other's nails, going to our favorite restaurants, showing me how to cook, or sitting at the shop with you, waiting for you to get off work. I always felt special and wanted.

As we grew older, so did our relationship. And although it changed, we changed. It has been rocky at times because of how close we are. Boundaries have been necessary for us as we continue to navigate life together and apart. Even still, I know that my mother is also my friend. Having children, moving states, cities, and towns, both of us having marriages and divorces... all of these things only brought us even closer.

Thank you.

While oversimplified, this is the greatest expression that I could think of to summarize my gratitude. I have an appreciation that is impossible to express through words. I believe this is why I work so hard to be a force of change in the world. Because, throughout my life, I display the love that I received from you. I feel a little closer to you and God through my small but mighty efforts. Not moved by the opinions of others but in service of others.

Over the years, my understanding of your sacrifices, heart, and true beauty has become clear. At times, I felt either intrusive or too much, but the lessons would have come 10 times harder without it. Your protection and presence served as a shield.

The intimate stories that you've shared to spare me from pain and heartache and how you continue to show up for my children and me. I wholeheartedly understand what motherhood looks like and feels like. We often want to break away from an undesirable warmth to grow independently, only to crave its comfort.

I've learned that motherhood is not a monolith, but a sea of potential, utilized to raise other beings and evolve as women ourselves.

We have grown together in so many ways. Witnessing the growth of my own mother has been an experience that not many may understand. As a young mom, you have grown into a "Honey" to all babies before my eyes. Sharing your food, wisdom, and love with all.

While your tenderness is not meant for all to understand, some even try to fight against it, I see you. I've always recognized the purity in the way that you love. The vulnerability that you seek in your interactions.

I'm here to tell you, it's not in vain.

The pride that has come from seeing the evolution of my mother has pushed me to not only assimilate to your example, but our closeness has also thrust me to new heights, hoping that my example will do the same for mine.

Without your selflessness and commitment to me over men, I formed a deep understanding of self. I saw a true example of "what is meant for me, will find me." I submitted to the calling of being a mommy while waiting for true companionship, respect, and quality to come my way.

I constantly hear, "you are so much like your mother," as I age. Beautiful words to my ears because MY MOTHER IS A QUEEN! You are a bold, outspoken, beautiful, powerful, kind, multitalented, deserving queen who continuously supports her community. You are a true healer through your skills as a hairstylist, cooking (did I say your FOOD), conversation, nurturing presence, and personality. Working to acknowledge the opportunities for growth that remain while standing strong in your knowing.

Your story has been the catalyst for generational change. Leading me and our future generations towards true freedom from the burden of trauma, repeated patterns of self-sacrifice, envy, substance abuse, and so much more. You have overcome so much. Without your fight, I cannot imagine what my boys and I would be fighting against today. Know that I will continue down this path of privilege, the privilege of being your daughter, and be prepared for any challenge that comes my way.

As I continue on my journey, I am often brought to tears because you are always right there when I turn to my side. Cheering me on, sharing my accomplishments with the world, even leading our youth together.

The change began with you and,
I THANK YOU, MA!

Love you deeply, always & forever.
Khris

"10,9,8,7,6,5,4,3,2,1 Breathe, You Got This"

By Monique Johnson

No one said it was going to be easy. We never had a family handbook handed down to help us be mothers. Instead, we learned from trial and error or what we know. Ever since I was little, I always said I would have four children — two girls and two boys — and I did. But no one prepared me for how hard it would be. I got married young, and even though I was married, I still felt like I was doing all this alone. My children were with me 24/7. So when I say I didn't experience my 20's, I didn't. I didn't start living until my 30s, and that was just a little.

As moms, we tend to forget about ourselves and need time to regroup. We're so eager to get everything done for others that we lose track of what we need and want for ourselves. So let me tell you a little secret: you can buy that bra you need because you haven't bought bras in years or a pair of shoes that you want and not feel guilty. After all, you haven't gotten anything for your children. It's okay. I had to realize that. I would feel so bad because I was thinking about myself and not my children. How dare I not put them first. But they weren't without clothes, toys, food, and everything. So why couldn't I be happy? I had to realize that it was something deeper. The things they went through as children, the isolation, divorce, the move - I felt was my fault. That I didn't deserve happiness. Unless they were happy.

I remember telling my mother, "When I get older and have children, I'm not going to treat them anything like you treat me," and I didn't. Instead, I chose to be a better mother and not follow in the same footsteps I was shown.

I loved being a new mother. I had all my children at home on a birthing chair. Many people asked me if I was scared to not be in a hospital. No, I trusted my midwives, and everything was just right. It was dim, lit with candles, light music played in the background. It was very calming. I don't know, but I felt when I held my first child was unexplainable. She was perfect, and I just cried because I did that. I pushed out a healthy baby girl.

After having my first child, I didn't feel alone because everyone wanted to see the baby. Still, they were worried about me and how I was doing that I didn't have time to dwell on my inner thoughts. Moving along a year and some months later, I had another girl, and I was happy because I wanted my first child to have someone to play with. I didn't know what it was to have siblings. It worked out that they did everything together, and they loved each other.

In the next three years, I had two miscarriages, and I thought maybe I was being punished because I wasn't doing a good job as a parent. I hit a real dark place. I was depressed, and all while I was smiling in people's faces, my house was a mess. I would hide box cakes from my husband. I would wait for him to go to work, bake a cake, eat the whole thing in one sitting, and clean up all the evidence like it never happened. This went on for over a year.

    Three years after having my second child, I was blessed with child number three. I didn't know what I was having with any of my children until I was literally pushing them out. At the beginning of this letter, I told you I've always wanted to have two girls and two boys. My midwives knew my girls drove me crazy by constantly fighting; they were a lot. So, when It was time to give birth, I waited until the very moment that when they got there, they set up everything, and I went and sat down on the chair, and they said, "Okay, you can push" and one push is all it took. I wanted to know what I was having even though I wanted a healthy baby overall. I cried overwhelmingly because I finally got my boy.

    Because of the birth of my children, I felt as though things were getting back on track for me. However, my marriage started to fall apart. I started thinking that if I couldn't be close to my husband, I needed another baby to hold on to and love to distract me from what I was really losing. So, I prayed for my fourth child, and I got pregnant. I was happy because I had my days full of children and working and growing a little one inside that I focused on.

    When the day came to give birth to my son, my mom was with me. Another mom was giving birth at the same time, so my midwives couldn't be there. They talked my mom through the process, and she got to experience me giving birth. It was a special moment.

    We did that.

And as I remained calm, I realized just how strong we are as women. I realized just how strong I was. I gave birth to four beautiful babies from this body. At that moment, I understood that there was nothing I could not do because I was a woman.

Don't ever let someone say you can't do anything. We are strong, resilient women who march to our own drums' beat and get stronger by the day.
Just remember, "10,9,8,7,6,5,4,3,2,1 breathe, you got this."

Love,
Monique Johnson

There Is Power In Asking For Help

By Patrice Hernandez

"Just breathe..." Those were the words I whispered to myself moments before the anesthesia took control of my body. I was terrified. This was the end of a chapter for me. "When I wake, it will be the beginning of a new chapter." Uncertain of what the future held for me on the next page, I drifted into a deep slumber. After surgery, I woke up feeling like a different woman. It may have been my subconscious speaking to me. I did not feel amazing or like the woman from the previous chapter. Could it be that I felt this way because I could no longer have children? I felt like the surgery was a blessing and a curse.

I would no longer live a life filled with pain. I would focus on my physical and mental well-being. Life would be great. I was wrong. Physically, I no longer had the option to have more children. My recovery process was not a classic textbook case. It was a book filled with new pain, challenges, and emotions.

Days passed...I felt weak, imperfect, damaged. I did not show up daily as the best version of myself. I did not know or understand how to give myself grace. I did not feel worthy. The feelings of sadness were overwhelming. Heartbreak, regret, mourning...There was no shortage of words to describe how I felt each day.

Seven days after my hysterectomy and one day after my birthday, I felt weird. It was akin to an out-of-body experience. I felt weak, tired, and nauseous. It was like nothing I had felt before. I called for my husband, Danny, and by the time he reached me, I was falling - not so gracefully to the floor. Unconscious, I am not sure how long I lay lifeless on the floor before the paramedics got to me.

Unsure of the time frame, I could hear my husband calling my name, and help was near. There was no way to respond, "I am here. I am alive." As paramedics pounded on my chest, I lay there telling myself to wake up. "Open your eyes! Wake up! Move! Do something." I could not do anything. After some time, I felt a pound, quickly opened my eyes and released a loud gasping sound. Perfect! I am alive. There was one problem, I could not move. Except for my eyes, I could not move any part of my body.

I was lifted onto a gurney and wheeled to the ambulance. As I entered the scary vehicle, I could see my husband crying. During this time, I did not see my Cheetahs (daughters). Instead, I could see the brightness of the interior of the ambulance. I recall the paramedic sitting and talking to me as I was transported to the hospital. Although I could not move or speak, he whispered to me. "I am here with you. It's going to be okay." Tears streamed down my cheeks. He grabbed something to wipe away my tears. His words caused me to cry even more. "Are you scared? Don't be afraid. We are going to help you."

The road trip to the hospital seemed to last an eternity. I spent a week away from home. It was a long week, filled with beeping noises, needles, and nurses. It took days before I gained mobility back in my body and even more days before I could speak. During my hospital stay, I was introduced to a speech therapist. Her job, of course, was to help me learn how to talk again. For some reason, I could not utter a word. I tried. My family attempted to help me as well. Finally, I could only sing the Happy Birthday song after some time.

Everyone would ask me questions and tell me to blink once for yes, two times for no. It was frustrating for me but helpful. I could not speak up for myself. Thank God my husband was there. He spent time advocating for me. One morning, one of my nurses came in to draw labs. Unable to find my veins, the nurse moved the needle around my arm and my hand. It was so painful that it left me in tears. My husband demanded that he stop.

After being released from the hospital, I regained my strength and voice. I felt like The Little Mermaid. I wanted to say so much but could only sign or write down what I wanted. But, all of that did not matter because I was home, in my safe haven.

My family, friends, and even strangers became my community of help. Once word spread, families were bringing us meals, keeping and teaching the girls (because they are homeschooled.) I felt helpless but blessed to have so many people rally around us. My Aunt Deborah made a visit to us. She was a welcomed help.

I spent more time with doctors than I would have liked. It took a long time to receive an actual diagnosis. What I experienced was a seizure. After regaining my speech and full mobility, I began having more seizures. Finding the right doctor was imperative to begin the healing process.

My first neurologist was not helpful. Since I am a Veteran, I was able to be seen at the VA. I found an incredible medical team there. I am still a patient with the same doctor. The treatment that I received has led me towards healing.

Let's talk about it...

My family endured my feelings. If Mom is not happy, then no one is happy. This sentiment rang true in our home that year. It is not a lovely feeling to see your family unhappy. I spent many nights crying until I could no longer produce tears, feeling defeated because I had lost a part of myself. This part could never be returned. Our little family of four was used to being independent. It was difficult for us to be vulnerable.

Over time, I realized that I had two options. I could wallow in sadness or be grateful for the two blessings in my life and for healing. I chose the latter. I wanted to be better. Happy. Healthy. My children deserved a mother who could be what they needed. I needed to heal from the past and from my illness. But unfortunately, I did not know how to heal.

Just breathe. Those words seemed to return to either haunt or help me. I took a deep breath and reached out to my doctor for help. I began meeting regularly with a counselor. I could have shared my feelings with those closest to me. But I needed more help navigating my feelings and thoughts than they could provide. I wanted the help without judgment.

Healing is a process. It takes time. Through counseling, I was capable of navigating my feelings. I can breathe. During the process, I learned a valuable lesson. It is okay to ask for help and allow others to help you. It is okay to have feelings about the inability to have children. There is power in asking for help. The beauty of flowing through the process allows for healing. Today, I have taken a moment to "Just breathe" and be grateful for my journey. I am fully present and aware that future chapters will be what I make of them. I choose to live in positivity and gratitude for those who I have been blessed with in my life. The journey of change has allowed me to let go, heal, and grow.

As moms, we tend to feel like we can do it all. The cleaning, shopping, working, taking care of our family, and everything in between. Many days, we are strong enough to handle it all. But, sometimes things become overwhelming, so much so that it affects our mental health. We cannot do it all. That is okay. Sometimes we get sick.

Mom, I want you to know it is *more* than okay to ask for help! Seems like such a novel idea, doesn't it?

Healing is within your reach...

As humans, we are filled with hope, love, and wonder. But, mom, asking for help is not just for you. When you open up your doors and your heart to allow others to help you, you create more of what this world needs, empathy.

You are teaching your children that hope is present and help comes in all forms. Our most beautiful lessons can be found when we ask for help. Let go of the burden of saying I can do it all.

There is power in asking for help. It is difficult because we do not want to feel like a charity case. It is easy to feel out of control when the world around you is falling apart. It may feel all-consuming. I know because I have been there. As a mother, we often face the struggle of feeling alone. Despite having a loving family and friends, we still think no one can understand.

Asking for help does not mean you are weak. The moments that we need assistance will show us that it is okay to ask. Take the time to honor your strengths and allow others to show you compassion and empathy. You are not selfish because you are asking for help.

Needing help can be presented in many forms, from making an appointment to meet with a counselor to having the desire to reconnect with your spouse by having a date night. There is support in your community. Introverted or extroverted, you can find that support you need by joining or building a community and connecting with others.

Embrace Your Village

By Thelma Jones

To the wonderful mothers in my life that I call Sunshine,

Thank you for trusting me enough to respect and learn from my motherhood journey. I remember when you told me you were pregnant and the joy I felt for being included in your journey. I feel blessed to have been included. I want you all to know that it's okay to lean on those around you. Please know that all mothers deserve help. Also, it's okay to accept help and take breaks for self-care. If you are not healthy mentally and physically, you cannot provide the best care for your babies. So Sunshine, don't forget to lean on your village.

While growing up, my mother had a village surrounding her. I spent plenty of time with my grandparents, aunts, and cousins. From what I have experienced, a village can be immediate family, friends, or those you are drawn to and feel safe around. I would definitely tell my younger self and you ladies to ask for help, listen to the advice given, and not be afraid to take a break. If I knew then what I know now, I would have listened more to those who were mothers before me without judgment or question. In most cases, we try to plan or gain insight as to what we should expect when expecting. In motherhood, I've found that incorporating different styles and advice from my village as they have grown has been my best tool.

Do you all remember the story of the day I thought I was grown? Eighteen years ago, I made the call to my mother that she was going to be a grandmother. I started the call with, "Mom, I have something to tell you, and remember that I am grown."

I feared her reaction but tried to act as grown as I could. After I dropped the bomb, she laughed and said, "Oh, you are grown, huh? Are you sure you are ready for this?" In years to come, she would use my infamous line on me whenever I had a concern or needed help. Just a little humor on her part. As you all may know, she was and still is supportive with a little fussing. With my rearing and her support, to this day, I am still big on the old saying, "it takes a village to raise a child."

I was raised to go for it all. I was so busy when my cousins had babies that I never babysat. I never learned how to feed a baby or care for one. So, when I became pregnant, I began to read books, ask questions, and watch VHS tapes (yes VHS) from the library to try and figure out this thing called motherhood.

The books, videos, advice, and doctors were very informative about being pregnant and giving birth but not thereafter. I read about the birth defects and all that could occur while pregnant and when giving birth, but I did not think in a million years that I would give birth three weeks early by an emergency c-section due to pre-eclampsia. My parents and brother were on a cruise and my boyfriend at the time was in another state for the Super Bowl. Subsequently, I was alone having a baby at 2 am in severe pain.

While being prepped to give birth, my aunt, grandmother, and my best friend showed up. At that precious moment, they were what I would call my village. Within two-and-a-half years, I had beautiful baby number two, again by c-section, which required more help with both babies while I healed. I was devastated to leave my toddler with family while I gave birth and recovered from my second c-section and a follow-up surgery a month later. My village surrounded me and stepped up again by allowing me to heal and feel safe.

Throughout my motherhood journey, I have asked the question many times, "Where is my village?" My village wore thin due to life events, disagreements, and changes; however, I was blessed with new additions to my village throughout this journey. My village has helped me through many trials and tribulations that kept my babies happy, healthy, and safe.

I've learned to trust as a mother because I'm a momma bear through and through. I had to open myself up to trusting family, friends, and caregivers with my precious babies. So, I will say to you ladies to do your research, watch the signs, ask the hard questions, and be open to allowing others to help. This way, you can take comfort in knowing you have done all you can to protect your babies. To my Sunshines who have lost family members that you considered key to your village, remember that you are not alone even though it gets rough. You still have a village surrounding you. So, before motherhood becomes exhausting, consider leaning on them and take a beat.

Evoke the thought of not feeling ashamed. Understand that taking a break and asking for help does not make you a bad mother. If you are not familiar with these tools yet, try to incorporate mediation, walking, yoga, stretching, deep breathing, or binaural beats as a form of self-care. Consider the rearing of your parents, family input, and friends when figuring out your style. As the world changes, you will be open to creative parenting styles to ensure that your babies are loved and survive.

Remember that I will always be here for you and my bonus babies. Whether near or far, I am just a phone call away. Don't let your strength, pride, nor hurts from the past keep you from embracing your village. Thank you all for being a part of my village.

Love,
Sunshine

A Love Note from Mom To J and K

By Jennifer Dungey

I remember sitting in my high school classroom and while others were dreaming about being doctors and architects, I sat there dreaming about becoming a mom. People might ask why. Did I come from a broken home? Absolutely not. My mother and my father were married, and I assume we were considered upper-middle class at the time. I went to a private school, I received a superior education, yet while I sat in that English literature class, the only thing that I could think of becoming was a mom.

Sometimes I wish I could journey back in time to my 15-year-old self and tell her, "Sis the dream does come true," but I let so many others tell me before I got there that the dream was silly or that it was stupid. "We are in the twentieth century. Women can work nowadays. Why would you just want to be a mother?" So I write this letter on why I chose to become Mother to J and K:

Dear J and K,

I love you with every breath in my body. From before I ever thought of you, God knew I was meant to be your mama. There were trials and tribulations, miscarriages before you both got here. Moments where I thought I had messed up so bad in life that it was not meant to be a mommy. I truly was lost in this world and, J, you saved me. We gave you a strong Biblical middle name because I wanted you to be a man full of love.

You showed me how to love more and be more selfless than I could ever be. You made me into the mama bear I am. Please know that I made mistakes along the way. I was not perfect. When you were created, I was set upon giving you the best life possible. You redeemed me. Sometimes we, as parents, think we are doing best by our children, but truly our children are the ones who save us. I will forever be grateful for the gift of becoming your mama.

You know, when you're pregnant, the funniest things concern you. Well for me, when I saw my ultrasound and found out it was a boy, I was *scared*. Big-crocodile-tears scared!

How was this single mom going to teach a boy to pee standing up?

KK you have been my twin. My heart piece. My reminder to breathe again. Your name means "sent from heaven," and you are just that. You came at a time when so much was happening. I literally almost lost my life giving birth to give life to you. You truly were a gift from heaven and a reminder to stop and smell the flowers.

I love you both with all of my heart.

Love,
Mom

Encouraging Letter To An Amazing Mom

By Sabia Williams

This letter comes in the form of encouragement as you walk through this special motherhood journey. Being a mom is such a blessing. I started real young as a mom, and my life has always revolved around my children and all of the things that made them happy.

I didn't have much, but I am grateful to my Lord for giving me the strength and courage to establish good and healthy principles that helped make a positive difference in their upbringing. I feel that they have proven to me to be all they can be by showing their gratitude as evidence for doing the best they can be in their lives. They haven't been perfect and had struggles like many others, but I have taught them never to give up and pursue their visions and dreams.

I believe that a mother's time is so precious when it comes to her children. To me, time with my children is like a precious pearl. Although they grew up to become adults, time spent with them cannot replace my time with me. "Time" is not your enemy; it is your friend. So what does time express to us as moms?

Let me share one of the many experiences I had while raising my three children when they were young. One day, one of my middle schoolers seemed sad when she came home from school. I was a little puzzled because I knew that I couldn't imagine her being bullied at school with her type of personality. As a helicopter mom, I have always been involved in their school activities. During that moment, I was ready to roll my sleeves up and say, "Oh no! What's up?" But instead, I gracefully greeted her with a smile, fixed her a snack, and started an open and closed conversation with her. My first question was, "How was your day?"

She opened up and shared her feelings about how unhappy she was about not fulfilling her dreams. Her dream was to become a professional artist. So I gave her the opportunity to share her art pieces with me, and OMG! They were so beautiful!

Her paintings were hidden behind her dresser in her room. She hid them because she thought they weren't good enough to share with others. The first piece was a cross-stitch of a bowl of fruit. The second piece was an image of a young girl hidden in her shadows. Speaking of time, as she began to share her vision with me, I invited her to join me while cooking a meal. While she was helping me chop up the onions, I could remember she seemed comfortable talking.

Sometimes when I think about that moment, I laugh about it because there was a funny part. We all know how onions can give teary eyes, and while she was sharing her feelings, she saw a waterfall of tears coming from my eyes.

Well, guess what? That was not the onions! Those were real tears! I wanted her to think it was only the onions because I did not want her to feel that I was sad or judging her. On the contrary, I was very happy with tears of joy that she opened the door and let me into her world. I supported her vision because I understood how she felt about her dreams. I understood the purpose of her paintings and encouraged her to create a plan that would help build an avenue to become successful in her future endeavor.

    A mother knows her children, and she knows their character traits. My youngest was such a quiet individual. I used to call her my voice of reason. If she thought my decisions about something were not logical, she would challenge me, and her favorite words were, "Mom.... are you sure?" Her quiet tone would allow me to think first before making what I thought was a good choice. For example, if I said to her, "I think we should spend time at the movies on Saturdays," she would say, "Mom, how about we just rent movies," or, "How about we spend time at the library on Saturdays?" I thought that was a terrific idea.

    When she grew older and graduated from high school, her interest was attending college and studying journalism as a major. I was surprised by her choice because of her prior interest in becoming a pediatrician. Living a college life and studying hard was not an easy task for her, but she never gave up, and she was able to cross over any obstacles until she completed her journey and graduated.

    My oldest reminds me of myself. She is modest, genuine, and a precious pearl that cannot be replaced. As my firstborn, this young lady has walked through many valleys with me, and her life is an epiphany of my life experience when I was a young mom. We spend time together on Saturdays for coffee and tea. I love hearing her genius views about life, and I love that she has blessed me with a wonderful son-in-law and three beautiful grandchildren. Her life truly exemplifies *Proverbs 31: 10* "Who can find a virtuous woman, she is worth far more than jewels." A trait which I feel very honored to say she has inherited.

You see, Moms, time is not only "the essence of life itself," but it is also something to value as your friend. She will sit and think with you, reason with you, comfort you, walk with you through your healing, and help you raise your children with blessed wisdom and divine guidance.
Time will help you stay focused on the most important things in your children's lives and reflect on yours. Time will allow you to slow down when moving too fast and move fast when moving too slow. She will help you keep the pace, and if you trip, fail, or fall, she will help you get back up again and start all over until you get it right. She will not hinder you unless you hinder yourself.

You are special, and although you wear many hats, turn the kitchen table around and treat yourself to a cup of coffee or tea, a book, relax and say to yourself, "It's my time."
Live, love, and be proud of yourself for doing the best you are doing and have done for yours. Regardless of how things may turn out, remember your labor is not in vain. The Lord will always bless you for having the heart to love your children and invite quality time to share with them. Those are moments that will never be forgotten. Save it in

your treasure box (your heart) as a reminder that your children matter and so do you. May the Lord bless you always.

All the best,
Sabia LaFleur-Williams

To The Mom Struggling With Working-Mom Guilt

By K. LaFleur-Anders

After experiencing a difficult delivery with my first son, Elijah, I wasn't sure if I wanted another baby. At least, that's what I tried to convince myself. I told myself I was done and I told my husband that too. I was fine with "practicing" but the thought of going through contractions and another C-section was a "no for me, dawg."

By the time Elijah was 5 years old, I was looking forward to him starting school so I could explore this new life we were establishing in Austin. I wasn't sure what kind of career I wanted here, but one in corporate America seemed like a no-brainer. There were tech companies everywhere, and everyone I met in Round Rock seemed to have worked for Dell so that's where I wanted to work, too.

So, here I was. Working in tech and aggressively pursuing a higher role from the very start. However, in my heart, I was ready for another baby. No matter how much I tried to tell myself I didn't, I did.

In 2011, morning sickness hit me like two tons of bricks, and instantly I knew. Although I felt horrible during the first trimester, I was so happy. I was happy that a sweet baby was on his/her way to my arms. Besides the first trimester, pregnancy with Isaiah was a breeze. He had his favorite spot in my belly and I would feel him moving all day. The visits to the OB were like field trips for me. I anticipated seeing an image of him as I tried to imagine what his cute little face would look like in real life. During every visit, he was running out of space in my belly. I just couldn't wait to hold and kiss him. I couldn't wait to see his face and smell his little baby feet. That's the best time to smell them, right?

    I remember waking up early in the morning and preparing to attend Elijah's first award ceremony at school. I was so excited! However, Isaiah had other plans. He was ready to meet the dog that barked at my stomach every time he moved. He was ready to wrestle with his dad who talked to him every day while poking at my stomach. He was ready to meet his brother who constantly made us laugh. He was ready to meet his mama.

    The day he was born was easier than the months I carried him. Besides the excruciating contractions that came before him, delivering Isaiah was so easy. He came out cool and ready for the world. It didn't take him very long to open his eyes. He was ready to see what was going on in the room. But unlike the time I was able to spend at home with Elijah, I knew that my time with Isaiah was limited. Maternity leave was not an option for me in the new role I pursued. I had to go back to work.

    Every day I went to work felt like my heart was ripping into pieces. I felt so guilty for leaving him every morning. He was with my mom every day, but *I* wanted to be with him. I cried about it often in private conversations with my husband and he always took that time to reassure me that I was an extraordinary mother. I didn't feel that way at all. Every time I saw Isaiah, I smothered him with so many hugs and kisses. Even though I was working outside of the home when he was a baby, the cuddles and kisses when I got home carried me through my most difficult days. I may have felt guilty about being at work, but coming home to flowers he picked for me at the park instantly made those feelings disappear. It was always a joy coming back to those chubby cheeks and huge smiles.

Today, Isaiah is a brave, intelligent, and fearless 10-year-old who loves me as much as I love him. He's generous with hugs and compliments, reminding me every day that he thinks I'm a great mom. He tells me, he shows me, and I feel it. Even on days when I feel like I'm failing, he reminds me that I don't have to be perfect for him to know I love him. He's my rock in many ways, even though he may be too young to understand why. It's like we never missed a beat with bonding, and that's because we didn't. Even after we left the hospital and after I returned to work, we kept bonding.

Eventually, Isaiah made me accept that the season we were in when he was born spoke volumes about where we needed to be to welcome him into our lives. He's taught me such beautiful lessons of faith and gratitude. His life is a gift and I'm so blessed to be his mom.

I was afraid that I was missing that bonding window that I heard about. You know, it's almost as if you're going to miss out on the most important moments in their lives if you don't bond with them all day while they are infants.

But the truth is, you have time. So breathe and let each moment captivate you. Be present when they are present and take it all in.

If you missed skin-to-skin, you can still give hugs. If you weren't able to spend months at home for some bonding time, you still have each day to create memories and to hold them tightly. If you're not at home during the day because you have to work, you still have time at night to read bedtime stories together. You still have moments to take and memories to make. Strengthen your bond every day. You still have time.

Made in the USA
Las Vegas, NV
16 September 2022